GREAT WALL CHINESE

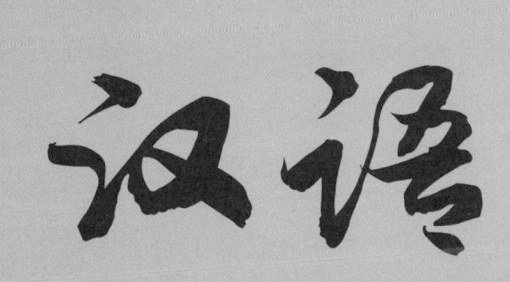

生存交际
Essentials in Communication

第2版
Second Edition

学生用书
Textbook

主编　马箭飞　宋继华

外语教学与研究出版社
FOREIGN LANGUAGE TEACHING AND RESEARCH PRESS
北京 BEIJING

图书在版编目 (CIP) 数据

长城汉语生存交际 1 学生用书：第 2 版：汉、英／马箭飞，宋继华主编 . -- 北京：外语教学与研究出版社，2020.12（2024.9 重印）
　　ISBN 978-7-5213-2281-1

Ⅰ. ①长… Ⅱ. ①马… ②宋… Ⅲ. ①汉语－对外汉语教学－教材 Ⅳ. ①H195.4

中国版本图书馆 CIP 数据核字 (2020) 第 261034 号

出 版 人　王　芳
项目负责　刘雪梅
责任编辑　刘雪梅
责任校对　杨　益
装帧设计　范晔文
出版发行　外语教学与研究出版社
社　　址　北京市西三环北路 19 号（100089）
网　　址　https://www.fltrp.com
印　　刷　北京捷迅佳彩印刷有限公司
开　　本　889×1194　1/16
印　　张　10
版　　次　2021 年 5 月第 1 版　2024 年 9 月第 4 次印刷
书　　号　ISBN 978-7-5213-2281-1
定　　价　79.00 元

如有图书采购需求，图书内容或印刷装订等问题，侵权、盗版书籍等线索，请拨打以下电话或关注官方服务号：
客服电话：400 898 7008
官方服务号：微信搜索并关注公众号"外研社官方服务号"
外研社购书网址：https://fltrp.tmall.com

物料号：322810001

编委会

主编
马箭飞　宋继华

副主编
毛　悦　高　新

编者
谭春健　梁彦民　刘长征
赵雪梅　王　枫　陈若君
张媛媛　王　轩　张一萍

练习编写
负责人　陈　军
赵秀娟　梁　菲　李先银
杨慧真　魏耕耘　李　泓

翻译
王培伦　高明乐　张　旭

故事、情景
张作民　卢岚岚

教学实验
负责人　迟兰英
毛　悦　赵秀娟　陈　军　魏耕耘
杨慧真　李　泓　袁金春

文字审核
周婉梅　刘雪梅　杨　益　崔　超
杨　飘　谭紫格　张俊睿

测试研发
负责人　谢小庆
彭恒利　鲁新民　姜德梧　任　杰
张晋军　李　慧　李桂梅

技术开发、技术支持
负责人　宋继华　许建红
北京长城汉语中心
北京汉雅天诚教育科技有限公司

前 言
PREFACE

"长城汉语"是原孔子学院总部/国家汉办规划、组织、研发、运营的重点项目,是基于网络多媒体技术开发、契合移动互联网与人工智能时代发展需要的国际中文教育资源与工具体系,是技术支持环境下的新型国际中文教学模式与服务平台。

"长城汉语"以培养学习者的汉语交际能力为主要目标,运用网络多媒体课件、面授、学生用书/练习册、移动APP等多元资源与学习方式,采用即时跟踪学习进度和测试学习效果的管理模式,依托丰富的教学资源,向学习者提供个性化的学习方案,以满足海内外汉语学习者任何时间、任何地点、任何水平的泛在学习需求。

《长城汉语》教材是"长城汉语"的重要组成部分,它完整体现了该教学模式的等级序列和学习内容。教材分为"生存交际""拓展交际"和"自由交际"三个阶段,既相互衔接,又各自独立;每个阶段包括6册学生用书,对应6个级别,每个级别包括10个单元。教材可以与教学/学习平台、多媒体课件、移动APP等配套使用,亦可独立使用,以支持课堂教学或自学。

《长城汉语》教材的内容设计以"创业""爱情""传奇""当代"四个故事为线索,话题涉及经济、文化、体育、伦理等领域,展现了当代中国社会生活的各个方面。以来自不同国家的留学生与他们的中国朋友等十几个人物的活动贯穿始终,人物个性鲜明,情节生动有趣且充满生活气息。课文内容将语言学习与故事情节有机地结合起来,语言真实、自然、地道、实用。

"生存交际"面向初级汉语学习者,内容涉及个人信息、生存交际、日常生活、学习工作、社会交往等多个话题,以解决学习者在日常生活中最基本的语言交际问题。

"长城汉语"的推广应用一直是采用半学术化方式推进的。自2005年2月起,经过验证性实验、推广性实验、孔子学院试用以及市场化推广,创新了大综合、大小课、讲练一复练、视听说、多媒体自学+面授辅导(翻转课堂)、游学、线上线下混合教学等多元教学模式,"长城汉语"产品形态也从最初的局域网、互联网、单机版拓展至如今的iPad、手机等移动设备,成为覆盖"教、学、管、测、评"的智能型服务性平台,取得了良好的应用效果。

为适应国际中文教育最新发展趋势,在广泛收集专家、用户以及市场各方面反馈意见的基础上,项目组对《长城汉语·生存交际》教材进行改版,补充语法、交际要点注释,配套文化点讲解,并修订了与时代发展不相适应的部分内容。同时,开发了以"长城汉语"为核心课程的"汉雅国际"汉语学习APP(学生端),通过整合优质学习资源,集成趣味学习工具,优化"班级圈""课程中心""分级阅读""识字""记词""动画配音""语典"等功能,学、记、听、练、测彼此融合,互联互通,共同构成了移动智能生态学习环境。

"长城汉语"的研发、应用、推广得到了北京语言大学、北京师范大学、北京外国语大学、中央民族大学、首都经济贸易大学、加拿大卡尔加里大学、美国肯尼索州立大学孔子学院、德国慕尼黑孔子学院、西班牙巴塞罗那孔子学院基金会等学校和机构以及诸多国内外专家的帮助和支持,是集体科研和智慧的结晶,在此一并表示衷心的感谢!

编者　2020年12月

人物介绍
CHARACTER INTRODUCTION

麦克　Mike

男，28岁，美国人，中国某大学来华留学生。热情、有活力，喜欢登山。课余担任某健身俱乐部教练。

Male, 28 years old, American. He is an international student of a university in China. He is warm-hearted and energetic, fond of mountaineering. He works in a fitness club as a coach in his spare time.

张芳芳　Zhang Fangfang

女，23岁，中国人，曾是某中医学院学生。活泼、开朗。大学毕业后在某医院工作。

Female, 23 years old, Chinese. She graduated from a college of traditional Chinese medicine. She is lively and cheerful. She works in a hospital after graduation.

张圆圆　Zhang Yuanyuan

女，23岁，中国人，张芳芳的双胞胎妹妹，曾是某大学中文系学生。善良、内向，喜欢登山。大学毕业后在某杂志社当编辑。

Female, 23 years old, Chinese. She is Zhang Fangfang's twin younger sister. She was a Chinese major in university. She is kind-hearted and introverted, fond of mountaineering. She works as an editor of a magazine after graduation.

Great Wall Chinese

菲雅　Faye

女，24岁，印尼人，《环球》杂志社记者。追求时尚，个性鲜明。在中国某大学学习汉语。

Female, 24 years old, Indonesian. She is a journalist of *The Globe*. She is fashionable with a strong character. She studies Chinese at a university in China.

陈晓红　Chen Xiaohong

女，25岁，中国人，中国某大学法语教师。温柔娴静。

Female, 25 years old, Chinese. She is a teacher of French at a university in China. She is gentle and refined.

李冬生　Li Dongsheng

男，30岁，中国人，中国某大学副教授、在读博士生。兴趣广泛、事业心强。爱好摄影、旅游等。

Male, 30 years old, Chinese. He is an associate professor of a university in China and a Ph.D. student. He has many interests and strong devotion to his work. He is fond of photography, traveling and so on.

Character Introduction

罗森 Rawson

男，25岁，法国人，中国某大学外籍教师。爱好音乐。

Male, 25 years old, French. He is a foreign teacher of a university in China. He is fond of music.

金太成 Kim Taesung

男，36岁，韩国人，韩国世纪数码公司设计部经理。成熟、稳重。边工作边在中国某大学学习汉语。

Male, 36 years old, South Korean. He is a manager of the design department in the South Korean Century Digital Company. He is mature and steady. He studies Chinese at a university while working in China.

山口和子 Yamaguchi Kazuko

女，27岁，日本人，日本某公司驻北京办事处的高级职员。温顺、谦和。边工作边在中国某大学学习汉语。

Female, 27 years old, Japanese. She is a senior clerk in the Beijing office of a Japanese company. She is meek and modest. She studies Chinese at a university while working in China.

Great Wall Chinese

王杨　Wang Yang

女，24岁，中国北京人，韩国世纪数码公司秘书。大方、干练。

Female, 24 years old, Chinese, a native of Beijing. She is a secretary in the South Korean Century Digital Company. She is decent, capable and experienced.

玛丽　Mary

女，22岁，英国人，中国某大学来华留学生。热情、开朗，爱好绘画。外婆是中国人。来中国寻找失散多年的外婆。

Female, 22 years old, British. She is an international student of a university in China. She is warm-hearted and cheerful, fond of painting. Her grandmother is Chinese. She came to China to look for her grandmother, whom she had been separated from and lost touch with for many years.

赵玉兰　Zhao Yulan

女，52岁，中国人，国家京剧院演员。热情、善良。擅长中国书法。

Female, 52 years old, Chinese. She is a performer in China National Peking Opera Company. She is warm-hearted and kind, and good at Chinese calligraphy.

刘少华　Liu Shaohua

男，56岁，中国人，赵玉兰的丈夫，作家。性情温和。爱好围棋和中国武术。

Male, 56 years old, Chinese. He is Zhao Yulan's husband and a writer. He has a gentle disposition. He is fond of playing go and kung fu.

爱德华　Edward

男，89岁，英国人，玛丽的外公。二战时期以记者的身份来到中国，结识了玛丽的外婆林雪梅并与其相爱，后来两人失散。

Male, 89 years old, British. He is Mary's grandfather. He came to China as a journalist during the Second World War. At that time he met Mary's grandmother Lin Xuemei and fell in love with her, but later they lost touch with each other.

林雪梅　Lin Xuemei

女，83岁，中国人，玛丽的外婆。年轻时当过护士。

Female, 83 years old, Chinese. She is Mary's grandmother. She used to be a nurse when she was young.

词性简称
ABBREVIATIONS OF PART OF SPEECH

名	名词	míngcí	noun
动	动词	dòngcí	verb
形	形容词	xíngróngcí	adjective
副	副词	fùcí	adverb
代	代词	dàicí	pronoun
介	介词	jiècí	preposition
连	连词	liáncí	conjunction
叹	叹词	tàncí	interjection
语气	语气词	yǔqìcí	modal particle
数	数词	shùcí	numeral
量	量词	liàngcí	measure word
助	助词	zhùcí	auxiliary word
缀	词缀	cízhuì	affix

Great Wall Chinese

目 录
CONTENTS

Title	Subject	Grammar points	Focal sentences	
Unit 1 你好，我是麦克。 Hello, I'm Mike. Page 1	Greetings	• Personal pronouns "你"(you), "我"(I/me), "他"(he/him), "她"(she/her), "您"(polite form of you), "你们"(plural form of you) • "是" sentence: introduction and description • The interrogative pronoun "谁"	我是张芳芳。 你好！ 您好！	他是谁？ 他是李老师。
Unit 2 我姓金，叫金太成。 My surname is Kim; full name is Kim Taesung. Page 13	Family names, given names	• Special questions with "什么" • General questions • The adverb "也"	对不起。 没关系。 您贵姓？ A：你叫什么名字？ B：我姓金，我叫金太成。	认识您很高兴。 我来介绍一下。
Unit 3 我从英国伦敦来。 I come from London, UK. Page 23	Nationality and place of someone's origin	• General questions with "吧" • Using "不" for negation • Special questions with "哪儿"or "什么地方" (both meaning "where")	请再说一遍。 请问，您是哪国人？ 谢谢！ A：你是哪国人？ B：我是日本人。	A：您是哪儿人？ B：我是北京人。 A：你是日本什么地方人？ B：我是日本东京人。 我从英国伦敦来。
Unit 4 我在一家公司工作。 I work for a company. Page 35	Occupations	• Measure words "个"，"名"，"家" • Adverbials of place • Adverbials of time • Noun/pronoun+的+noun	A：你做什么工作？ B：我是教练。 A：你在哪儿工作？ B：我在一家韩国公司工作。	对，我也工作。 不，我每天下午工作。 我喜欢这个工作。 我喜欢画画。
Unit 5 你今年多大？ How old are you? Page 47	Age	• Special questions with "几" (indicating quantity) • Noun-predicate sentences • The use of numerals • Reduplication of verbs	A：你今年几岁（了）？ B：我四岁（了）。 A：你今年多大（了）？ B：我21岁。 A：您今年多大年纪（了）？ B：我65岁了。	你星期六上午来，可以吗？/好吗？ A：您认识这个人吗？ B：我（不）认识这个人。
Unit 6 她的男朋友很帅！ Her boyfriend is very handsome! Page 59	One's figure and features	• Alternative questions • Questions with "多+adjective" • Affirmative-negative questions • Sentences with adjectival predicates and adverbs of degree	A：他帅不帅？ B：他很帅。 你想找这样的男朋友吗？ 她1米65。 我体重54公斤。	

Contents

Communication points	Words and phrases	Chinese characters	Culture corner
• Introducing one's name • Common greeting • Respectful greeting • Introducing or identifying others	你 好 我 是 您 你们 她 谁 他 老师 刘少华 赵玉兰 麦克 张芳芳 张圆圆 金太成 山口和子 王杨 玛丽 菲雅 李冬生 陈晓红	你 好 我 是 您 们 她 谁 他 老 师	你好 Hello!
• Basic ways to ask and tell someone's name	姓 叫 什么 名字 对不起 没关系 嗯 学生 吗 贵姓 请问（请、问） 认识 很 高兴 也 来 介绍 一下	姓 叫 什 么 名 字 对 不 起 没 关 系 嗯 学 生 吗 贵 请 问 认 识 很 高 兴 也 来 介 绍 一 下	姓名 Names
• Basic ways to ask and tell someone's origin	从 来 姓名 国籍 再 说 一 遍 哪 国 人 哦 的 护照 给 谢谢 吧 不 爸爸 妈妈 地方 但 罗森 法国 美国 英国 日本 韩国 北京 上海 广东 东京 伦敦 中国	从 国 籍 再 说 遍 哪 人 哦 的 护 照 给 谢 吧 不 爸 妈 地 方 但 北 京 中	北京 Beijing
• Affirming or negating questions or opinions of others	家 公司 工作 大家 教练 护士 名 大学生 秘书 好 每天（每、天） 图书馆 下午 在 哪儿 部门经理（部门、经理） 做 职员 记者 喜欢 这个 现在 画 啊 个 画家 珍妮 澳大利亚 德国	公 司 工 作 大 家 教 练 护 士 秘 书 每 天 图 书 馆 午 在 部 门 经 理 做 职 员 记 者 喜 欢 这 个 现 画 啊	上海 Shanghai
• Asking a child's age • Asking an adult's age • Asking a senior's age	今年 多大（多、大） 小朋友 几 岁 猜 对 阿姨 这 秘密 事 想 健身 女 星期六 上午 可以 大妈 京剧 声音 真 好听 年纪 外婆 看 李明	今 多 小 朋 友 几 岁 猜 对 阿 姨 秘 密 事 想 健 身 女 星 期 六 上 可 以 剧 声 音 真 听 纪 外 婆 看	年龄 Age
• Asking about someone's height	男朋友 帅 怎么样 不错 外国人（外国） 大学 学习 男 还是 个子 高 米 左右 找 这样 小姐 累 明天 休息 要 太 胖 啊 体重 公斤 还 可以 那时 漂亮 外公 汉语	男 帅 怎 样 错 习 还 子 米 左 右 找 样 姐 太 累 明 天 休 息 要 太 胖 体 重 公 斤 那 时 漂 亮 汉 语	长江 The Yangtze River

www.greatwallchinese.com 11

Title	Subject	Grammar points	Focal sentences
Unit 7 我住在阳光小区。 I live in Yangguang Residential Neighborhood. Page 71	Address	• The use of ordinal numbers • The expression of direction and position • The structure of "A+离+B+远/近"	A：你住在哪儿？　　　A：第二医院离这儿远不 B：我住在阳光小区24号　B：不太远。 　　楼17层1708号。　　　别客气。 明天见。 一会儿见。
Unit 8 我喜欢大家庭。 I like an extended family. Page 85	Family	• "了" at the end of a sentence • The expression of "only": 只有 • "有" sentences indicating possession • Using "和……一起"(together with…) and "一个人"(alone) as adverbial modifiers	A：你家（有）几口人？ B：我家（有）四口人。 我爸爸希望我去银行工作。 这个小区真漂亮。 真是个大家庭。
Unit 9 我最近很忙。 I've been very busy recently. Page 99	Time	• Point in time +"了" • Questions with "几点"(what time) and "什么时候"(when) • Adverbials of time: point in time+verb phrase; point in time+ 以前(before)/以后(after)+verb phrase	A：现在几点？ B：现在10点20。 请问，现在几点？ 对不起，几点了？ 劳驾，第二医院在哪儿？ 我每天6点起床。 不一定。
Unit 10 我来介绍一下。 Let me introduce. Page 113	Basic personal information	• Sentences with adjectival predicates	我来介绍一下。这是麦克， 我的健身教练。这是我姐姐张芳芳。 我们星期三下午3点半去健身。 我住在6号楼433房间。 你什么时候有时间？

课文翻译　TRANSLATION OF TEXTS　　Page 124
词语表　VOCABULARY LIST　　Page 132

Contents

Communication points	Words and phrases	Chinese characters	Culture corner
• Asking or telling someone's address • Bidding farewell	住 我们 学校 有 健美操 比赛 参加 当 去 宿舍 号 楼 房间 电话 见 喂 家 里 今天 晚上 宴会 饭店 接 小区 层 前边 等 一会儿 第二（第、二）医院 路 离 这儿 远 知道 东边 别客气 （别、客气） 阳光小区 长安饭店 第二医院 东城路	住 校 有 美 操 比 赛 参 加 当 去 宿 舍 号 楼 房 间 电 话 见 喂 里 晚 宴 会 饭 店 接 区 层 前 边 等 医 院 路 离 远 知 道 东 别 客 气	黄河 The Yellow River
• Inquiring about and introducing family members	家庭 口 四 妹妹 和 律师 非常 忙 常常 希望 银行 可是 医生 兄弟姐妹（兄弟、姐妹） 只 孩子 呢 姐姐 双胞胎 前面 就 送 父母 一起 都 爷爷 奶奶 哥哥 嫂子 他们 一共	庭 口 四 妹 和 律 常 忙 希 望 银 医 生 兄 弟 只 孩 呢 双 胞 胎 面 送 父 母 起 都 爷 奶 哥 嫂 共	家庭生活 Family Life
• Courtesy to make inquires • Asking for someone's opinions • Polite refusal	最近 点 半 劳驾 分 姑娘 差 愿意 能 时候 下班 行 到 吃 晚饭 开始 训练 先生 起床 以后 睡觉 这么 上班 加班 总公司 项 重要 不一定 有时候 星期五 有空儿 再说	最 近 点 半 劳 驾 分 姑 娘 差 愿 意 能 候 班 行 到 吃 饭 开 始 训 练 先 床 以 后 睡 觉 加 总 项 重 定 五 空 再	烤鸭 Roast Duck
• Expressing the time	真的 没什么 欢迎 下次（下、次） 星期三 好的 朋友 女儿 学 教 时间 没有 课 给 打	真 迎 次 三 教 间 课 打	汉字 Chinese Characters

UNIT 1

Nǐ hǎo, wǒ shì Màikè.
你好，我是麦克。
Hello, I'm Mike.

Objectives

In this unit, you'll learn:
- the basic ways to greet people in Chinese
- to tell someone your Chinese name and the name of others

Great Wall Chinese

学习要点 | Key Points

Subject	Greetings	
Goals	Learn the basic ways to greet people in Chinese, and to tell someone your Chinese name and the name of others	
Grammar points	• Personal pronouns "你"(you), "我"(I/me), "他"(he/him), "她"(she/her), "您"(polite form of you), "你们"(plural form of you) • "是" sentence: introduction and description • The interrogative pronoun "谁"	
Focal sentences	Introducing one's name	我是张芳芳。
	Common greeting	你好!
	Respectful greeting	您好!
	Identifying someone	他是谁?
	Introducing someone	他是李老师。
Words and phrases	你 好 我 是 您 你们 她 谁 他 老师 刘少华 赵玉兰 麦克 张芳芳 张圆圆 金太成 山口和子 王杨 玛丽 菲雅 李冬生 陈晓红	
Chinese characters	你 好 我 是 您 们 她 谁 他 老 师	

第 1 课 LESSON ONE

课文 | Text 🎧 1-1

Liú Shàohuá	Wǒ shì Liú Shàohuá.
刘 少 华	我是刘少华。

Zhào Yùlán	Wǒ shì Zhào Yùlán.
赵 玉 兰	我是赵玉兰。

Mài kè	Wǒ shì Màikè.
麦 克	我是麦克。

Zhāng Fāngfāng	Wǒ shì Zhāng Fāngfāng.
张 芳 芳	我是张芳芳。

Zhāng Yuányuan	Wǒ shì Zhāng Yuányuan.
张 圆 圆	我是张圆圆。

Jīn Tàichéng	Wǒ shì Jīn Tàichéng.
金 太 成	我是金太成。

Shānkǒu Hézǐ	Wǒ shì Shānkǒu Hézǐ.
山 口 和 子	我是山口和子。

Wáng Yáng	Wǒ shì Wáng Yáng.
王 杨	我是王杨。

Mǎ lì	Wǒ shì Mǎlì.
玛 丽	我是玛丽。

Fēi yǎ	Wǒ shì Fēiyǎ.
菲 雅	我是菲雅。

Lǐ Dōngshēng	Wǒ shì Lǐ Dōngshēng.
李 冬 生	我是李冬生。

Chén Xiǎohóng	Wǒ shì Chén Xiǎohóng.
陈 晓 红	我是陈晓红。

www.greatwallchinese.com

生词 | New Words 🎬1-2

1	我	wǒ	代	I, me
2	是	shì	动	to be

专有名词 | Proper Nouns

3	刘少华	Liú Shàohuá		Liu Shaohua
4	赵玉兰	Zhào Yùlán		Zhao Yulan
5	麦克	Màikè		Mike
6	张芳芳	Zhāng Fāngfāng		Zhang Fangfang
7	张圆圆	Zhāng Yuányuan		Zhang Yuanyuan
8	金太成	Jīn Tàichéng		Kim Taesung
9	山口和子	Shānkǒu Hézǐ		Yamaguchi Kazuko
10	王杨	Wáng Yáng		Wang Yang
11	玛丽	Mǎlì		Mary
12	菲雅	Fēiyǎ		Faye
13	李冬生	Lǐ Dōngshēng		Li Dongsheng
14	陈晓红	Chén Xiǎohóng		Chen Xiaohong

语法 | Grammar

1 人称代词 "你" "我" "他/她" "您" "你们"
Personal pronouns "你" (you), "我" (I/me), "他" (he/him), "她" (she/her), "您" (polite form of you), "你们" (plural form of you)

人称代词是用来指示或称代人的词语，语法功能跟名词相似。

Personal pronouns stand in place of nouns representing a person. Their grammatical function is similar to that of a noun.

Nǐ hǎo!
1 你好！
Hello!

Tā shì Zhāng Fāngfāng.
2 她是张芳芳。
She is Zhang Fangfang.

2 "是"字句：介绍与说明
"是" sentence: introduction and description

"是"字句主要用于介绍和说明。肯定形式是"主语+是+宾语"，否定形式是"主语+不是+宾语"，疑问形式是"主语+是+宾语+吗"。

"是" sentence is mainly used for introduction and description. Its affirmative form is "subject+是+object", negative form is "subject+不是+object" and interrogative form is "subject+是+object+吗".

Wǒ shì Màikè.
1 我是麦克。
I'm Mike.

Tā shì Lǐ lǎoshī.
2 他是李老师。
He's Teacher Li.

交际要点 | Communication Points

1 介绍自己的姓名
Introducing one's name

Wǒ shì Zhāng Fāngfāng.
我是张芳芳。
I am Zhang Fangfang.

中国人表达姓名的方式与一些欧美国家不同，中国人习惯将姓氏放在前面，名字放在后边。例如："张芳芳"，"张"是姓氏，"芳芳"是名字。

Unlike in some European and American countries, the family name comes before the given name in China. For example, in the name of "Zhang Fangfang", "Zhang" is the family name, and "Fangfang" is the given name.

第 2 课 LESSON TWO

课文 | Text

留学生报到处。 ▶1-3
At the registration office for international students.

Màikè	Nǐ hǎo!	Wǒ shì Màikè.	
麦克	你好！我是麦克。		
Jīn Tàichéng	Nǐ hǎo!	Wǒ shì Jīn Tàichéng.	
金太成	你好！我是金太成。		
Mǎlì	Nín hǎo!	Wǒ shì Mǎlì.	
玛丽	您好！我是玛丽。		
Fēiyǎ	Nín hǎo!	Wǒ shì Fēiyǎ.	
菲雅	您好！我是菲雅。		

在教室。
In the classroom.

Lǐ Dōngshēng   Nǐmen hǎo!   Wǒ shì Lǐ Dōngshēng.
李冬生　　　你们好！我是李冬生。

6　GREAT WALL CHINESE, A SIMPLE STEP TO SUCCESS!

生词 | New Words 🔊 1-4

1	你	nǐ	代	you
2	好	hǎo	形	well, good
3	您	nín	代	you (polite form)
4	你们	nǐmen	代	you (plural form)

交际要点 | Communication Points

2. 常用问候语
Common greeting

Nǐ hǎo!
你好！
Hello!

"你好"是汉语中最常用的问候方式，可用于一天当中的任何时间，其回答方式同样是"你好"。

"你好" is the most common greeting in Chinese and it can be used at any time of a day; the proper response is also "你好".

3. 尊称问候语
Respectful greeting

Nín hǎo!
您好！
Hello!

"您好"用于表达问候，比"你好"更礼貌，一般用于下级对上级或晚辈对长辈。有时初次见面，为了表示礼貌，也会用"您好"。

"您好" is also a common greeting in Chinese; however it is much more polite than "你好". It is commonly used to greet people who occupy a superior status to oneself, or to greet one's elders. "您好" is also used when meeting someone for the first time to show politeness.

第 3 课　LESSON THREE

课文 | Text

教室里。 ▶1-5
In the classroom.

Mài kè	麦 克	Nǐ hǎo! Wǒ shì Màikè. 你好！我是麦克。
Mǎ lì	玛 丽	Nín hǎo! Wǒ shì Mǎlì. 您好！我是玛丽。

菲雅走进教室。
Faye comes into the classroom.

Mài kè	麦 克	Tā shì shéi? 她是谁？
Mǎ lì	玛 丽	Tā shì Fēiyǎ. 她是菲雅。
Mài kè	麦 克	Fēiyǎ, nǐ hǎo! 菲雅，你好！
Fēi yǎ	菲 雅	Nǐ hǎo! 你好！

李冬生走进教室。
Li Dongsheng comes into the classroom.

Lǐ Dōngshēng	李 冬 生	Nǐmen hǎo! 你们好！
Mǎ lì	玛 丽	Tā shì shéi? 他是谁？
Fēi yǎ	菲 雅	Tā shì Lǐ lǎoshī. 他是李老师。
Mǎ lì	玛 丽	Lǎoshī, nín hǎo! Wǒ shì Mǎlì. 老师，您好！我是玛丽。
Mài kè	麦 克	Lǎoshī, wǒ shì Màikè. 老师，我是麦克。
Lǐ Dōngshēng	李 冬 生	Nǐ hǎo, Màikè! Nǐ hǎo, Mǎlì! 你好，麦克！你好，玛丽！

Unit 1 Lesson Three

生词 | New Words 🔊 1-6

1	她	tā	代	she, her
2	谁	shéi	代	who
3	他	tā	代	he, him
4	老师	lǎoshī	名	teacher

语法 | Grammar

3. 疑问代词"谁"
The interrogative pronoun "谁"

疑问代词"谁"用于询问人。
The interrogative pronoun "谁" is used to ask about a person.

Tā shì shéi?
A：她是谁？
Who is she?

Tā shì Fēiyǎ.
B：她是菲雅。
She is Faye.

交际要点 | Communication Points

4. 介绍或确认他人身份
Introducing or identifying others

Tā shì Lǐ lǎoshī.
他是李老师。
He is Teacher Li.

在中文里，当描述人们的身份与职务时，通常会把姓氏放在前边，把表示身份与职务的词放在后边，如"李老师""金经理"。有时也会用全名，如"张芳芳女士"。

In Chinese, when describing someone's identity and post, the usual way is to use his/her family name, followed by a word representing his/her identity or post, such as "李老师"(Teacher Li), "金经理"(Manager Kim). Sometimes, a person's full name may also be used, for example "张芳芳女士"(Ms Zhang Fangfang).

文化园 | Culture Corner

Hello!

"你好" is the most common expression for meeting someone in China, and can be used to greet people no matter whether they are friends, acquaintances or strangers. In most situations, "你好" is used to convey a sense of politeness or greeting. When you have a question that you would like to be answered, "你好" can also be used to start a dialogue. If the person you are addressing is an elder, or simply someone that you want to convey special respect to, you can say "您好", instead. Following "你好", you can add a lot of different expressions to add a personal touch to your greeting, such as "你好,最近身体好吗?" (Hello, has your health been well lately?), "你好,工作忙吗?" (Hello, has your work been busy?). "好" is the most effective way for Chinese people to convey a simple, down-to-earth sense of courtesy towards others; it is a way to express hope that the other person will smoothly stride towards their aspirations. The character "好" can be inserted after any form of address, such as "老师好" (hello teacher), "爷爷好、奶奶好" (hello grandpa, hello grandma), "叔叔好、阿姨好" (hello uncle, hello aunt), and so on. "好" has become a common language that Chinese people use to greet each other.

"你好"是中国人最常用的招呼用语,对认识的人、不认识的人,都可以说"你好"。一般情况下,"你好"只表达单纯的礼貌或者问候,当你有问题向别人请教时,也可以用"你好"做开场。如果对方是长者,或者是你比较尊敬的人,你可以说"您好"。在"你好"的后边,也可以根据情境表达个性化的内容,如"你好,最近身体好吗?""你好,工作忙吗?"等。"好"是中国人朴素待人礼节的最好体现,表达了希望对方一切顺利的愿望。"好"字可以加在任何一个称谓词的后面,如"老师好""爷爷好、奶奶好""叔叔好、阿姨好"等。"好"已经成为中国人相互表达问候的通用语。

生词复习 | Vocabulary Review

1	好	hǎo	well, good
2	老师	lǎoshī	teacher
3	你	nǐ	you
4	你们	nǐmen	you (plural form)
5	您	nín	you (polite form)
6	谁	shéi	who
7	是	shì	to be
8	他	tā	he, him
9	她	tā	she, her
10	我	wǒ	I, me
11	陈晓红	Chén Xiǎohóng	Chen Xiaohong
12	菲雅	Fēiyǎ	Faye
13	金太成	Jīn Tàichéng	Kim Taesung
14	李冬生	Lǐ Dōngshēng	Li Dongsheng
15	刘少华	Liú Shàohuá	Liu Shaohua
16	玛丽	Mǎlì	Mary
17	麦克	Màikè	Mike
18	山口和子	Shānkǒu Hézǐ	Yamaguchi Kazuko
19	王杨	Wáng Yáng	Wang Yang
20	张芳芳	Zhāng Fāngfāng	Zhang Fangfang
21	张圆圆	Zhāng Yuányuan	Zhang Yuanyuan
22	赵玉兰	Zhào Yùlán	Zhao Yulan

* The colored words are proper nouns.

UNIT 2

Wǒ xìng Jīn, jiào Jīn Tàichéng.

我姓金，叫金太成。

My surname is Kim; full name is Kim Taesung.

Objectives

In this unit, you'll learn:
- to ask and tell someone's family name
- to ask and tell someone's given name

学习要点 | Key Points

Subject	Family names, given names
Goals	Learn to ask and tell someone's family name and given name
Grammar Points	• Special questions with "什么" • General questions • The adverb "也"
Focal Sentences	Apologizing — 对不起。
	Responding to an apology — 没关系。
	Basic ways to ask and tell someone's name — 您贵姓? A: 你叫什么名字? B: 我姓金，我叫金太成。
	Greetings on the first meeting — 认识您很高兴。
	Announcing that you will make the introductions — 我来介绍一下。
Words and Phrases	姓 叫 什么 名字 对不起 没关系 嗯 学生 吗 贵姓 请问（请、问） 认识 很 高兴 也 来 介绍 一下
Chinese Characters	姓 叫 什么 名 字 对 不 起 没 关 系 嗯 学 生 吗 贵 请 问 认 识 很 高 兴 也 来 介 绍 一 下

14　GREAT WALL CHINESE, A SIMPLE STEP TO SUCCESS!

第 1 课 LESSON ONE

课文 | Text

公寓大厅。金太成走进来。
At the lobby of an apartment building. Kim Taesung comes in.

Jīn Tàichéng	Nǐmen hǎo.
金 太 成	你们好。
Màikè、Mǎlì	Nǐ hǎo!
麦克、玛丽	你好！
Mǎ lì	Nǐ shì …?
玛 丽	你是……？
Mài kè	Tā shì Jīn Tàichéng.
麦 克	他是金太成。
Jīn Tàichéng	Nǐ jiào shénme míngzi?
金 太 成	你叫什么名字？
Mǎ lì	Wǒ jiào Mǎlì.
玛 丽	我叫玛丽。

生词 | New Words 🔊 2-2

1	叫	jiào	动	to be called as
2	什么	shénme	代	what
3	名字	míngzi	名	name

语法 | Grammar

1 用"什么"的特殊疑问句
Special questions with "什么"

　　由疑问代词"什么"构成的疑问句，语序与陈述句相同，但句尾不用"吗"。"什么"用在指物或指人的名词前，询问事物的性质或人的职务、身份等，在句子里可以做主语或宾语。

　　An interrogative sentence that contains the interrogative pronoun "什么" has the same word order as a declarative sentence, and does not end with "吗". "什么" is placed before a noun representing an object or a person. It is used to ask the nature of something, the title or identity of someone and so on. It can be used as a subject or an object in a sentence.

Nǐ jiào shénme míngzi?
1 你叫 什么名字？
What's your name?

Tā xìng shénme?
2 她姓 什么？
What's her surname?

第 2 课 LESSON TWO

课文 | Text

图书馆门口,金太成不小心碰掉了山口和子的书。

At the entrance to the library, Kim Taesung bumped against Yamaguchi Kazuko accidentally and knocked the books out from her arms.

Jīn Tàichéng	Duìbuqǐ!	
金太成	对不起!	
Shānkǒu Hézǐ	Méi guānxi. Ńg… Nǐ shì xuéshēng ma?	
山口和子	没关系。嗯……你是学生吗?	
Jīn Tàichéng	Wǒ shì xuéshēng.	
金太成	我是学生。	
Shānkǒu Hézǐ	Nín guìxìng?	
山口和子	您贵姓?	
Jīn Tàichéng	Wǒ xìng Jīn, wǒ jiào Jīn Tàichéng. Qǐngwèn, nǐ jiào shénme míngzi?	
金太成	我姓金,我叫金太成。请问,你叫什么名字?	
Shānkǒu Hézǐ	Wǒ jiào Shānkǒu Hézǐ.	
山口和子	我叫山口和子。	
Jīn Tàichéng	Rènshi nǐ hěn gāoxìng.	
金太成	认识你很高兴。	
Shānkǒu Hézǐ	Rènshi nǐ wǒ yě hěn gāoxìng.	
山口和子	认识你我也很高兴。	

生词 | New Words

1	对不起	duìbuqǐ		I'm sorry
2	没关系	méi guānxi		it doesn't matter
3	嗯	ńg	叹	eh (expressing question)
4	学生	xuéshēng	名	student
5	吗	ma	语气	(a particle used at the end of a question)
6	贵姓	guìxìng		(your) surname (honorific)
7	姓	xìng	动	to be surnamed
8	请问	qǐngwèn	动	may I ask…
	请	qǐng	动	please
	问	wèn	动	to ask
9	认识	rènshi	动	to know
10	很	hěn	副	very, quite
11	高兴	gāoxìng	形	happy
12	也	yě	副	too, also, as well

语法 | Grammar

2 一般疑问句
General questions

表示疑问。一般由陈述句和句末语气词"吗"构成。用肯定或否定形式来回答。

"吗" is often used when asking someone a question. Generally speaking, "吗" will be put at the end of a statement. It can be responded to either affirmatively or negatively.

① Nǐ shì xuéshēng ma?
你是学生吗？
Are you a student?

② Nǐ shì Lǐ lǎoshī ma?
你是李老师吗？
Are you Teacher Li?

3 副词"也"
The adverb "也"

表示与前边提到的情况相同。结构是"主语+也+谓语"。

It denotes that the situation is same as what was mentioned previously. The structure is "subject+也+predicate".

Rènshi nín wǒ yě hěn gāoxìng.
认识您我也很高兴。
I'm also very happy to meet you.

交际要点 | Communication Points

问答姓名的基本方式
Basic ways to ask and tell someone's name

① Nín guìxìng?
您贵姓？
What's your surname?

"贵姓"用来礼貌地询问他人姓氏。在中国，一般初次见面只问姓氏要比询问全名更加礼貌，一般"贵姓"前面只能用第二人称"您"。

"贵姓" is used to ask someone's family name in a polite manner. In China, it is more polite to ask someone's family name instead of his/her full name on the first meeting. In general, only the pronoun "您" can be added before "贵姓".

② Nǐ jiào shénme míngzi?
A：你叫什么名字？
What is your name?

Wǒ jiào Mǎlì.
B：我叫玛丽。
I'm Mary.

"叫什么名字"用来询问他人的名字。在日常生活中，人们通常会告知自己的全名，即"姓氏+名字"，如"我叫李冬生"。

"叫什么名字" is used to ask someone's full name. In daily life, people usually tell their full names, for example "我叫李冬生" (My name is Li Dongsheng).

第 3 课 LESSON THREE

课文 | Text

校园餐厅内。玛丽和金太成正在吃饭，菲雅走进来了。 ▶2-5

At the cafeteria on campus. Mary and Kim Taesung are having their meal when Faye comes in.

Fēi yǎ	Nǐ hǎo, Mǎlì!	
菲 雅	你好，玛丽！	
Mǎ lì	Nǐ hǎo!	
玛 丽	你好！	
Jīn Tàichéng	Tā jiào shénme míngzi?	
金 太 成	她叫什么名字？	
Mǎ lì	Fēiyǎ. Wǒ lái jièshào yíxià.	
玛 丽	菲雅。我来介绍一下。	
	Tā jiào Fēiyǎ.	
	她叫菲雅。	
	Tā xìng Jīn, jiào Jīn Tàichéng.	
	他姓金，叫金太成。	
Fēi yǎ	Rènshi nín hěn gāoxìng.	
菲 雅	认识您很高兴。	
Jīn Tàichéng	Rènshi nín wǒ yě hěn gāoxìng.	
金 太 成	认识您我也很高兴。	

生词 | New Words ▶2-6

1	来	lái	动	(used before a verb or a verbal expression, indicating an intended action)
2	介绍	jièshào	动	to introduce
3	一下	yíxià		one time, once (used after a verb as its complement, indicating an act or an attempt)

文化园 | Culture Corner

中国约有14亿人口,常见的姓有几百个。中国人的姓名有三个特点。

1. 姓在前,名在后。无论男孩、女孩,一般都随爸爸的姓,女孩结婚后也不会改随夫姓。"姓"有单姓和复姓之分,如"刘少华",单姓"刘",名"少华";"诸葛亮",复姓"诸葛",名"亮"。

2. 除了在正式场合使用的姓名之外(中国人称"大名"),不少中国人小时候会有非正式的名字(中国人称"小名")。小名多在家庭和亲朋好友之间使用,长大以后一般不用。

3. 中国人的姓名不仅仅是人与人之间的区别符号,还蕴含了极其丰富的内涵,反映了家族的文化素养和价值取向。从不同的名字中,我们能感受到父母的期盼、家族的追求及情调。

Names

China has a population of around 1.4 billion and hundreds of common surnames. There are three characteristics of Chinese names.

1. A person's surname comes first, followed by his/her given name. Regardless of whether a child is a boy or a girl, he/she will typically receive the father's surname. When a girl gets married, she generally does not change her surname. A surname can be either a single character or a two-character compound. For example, the name "刘少华"(Liú Shàohuá) is comprised of the single-character surname "刘"(Liú) and the given name "少华"(Shàohuá), while the name "诸葛亮"(Zhūgě Liàng) contains the two-character compound surname "诸葛"(Zhūgě) and the given name "亮"(Liàng).

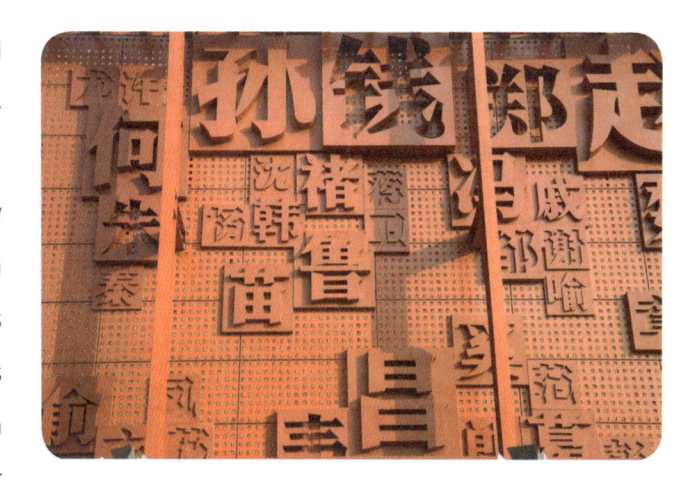

2. Apart from the name used on formal occasions (which is called as "大名" by Chinese people), some Chinese people have an informal name in their childhood (which is called as "小名"). A person's "小名" is usually used by his/her family, relatives and close friends, and is not used after he/she grows up.

3. Chinese surnames are much more than a way to differentiate people. A name carries with it rich connotations regarding the cultural accomplishments and values of the family. A given name can convey the expectations of parents and the pursuits and the sentiment of the family.

生词复习 | Vocabulary Review

#			
1	对不起	duìbuqǐ	I'm sorry
2	高兴	gāoxìng	happy
3	贵姓	guìxìng	(your) surname (honorific)
4	很	hěn	very, quite
5	叫	jiào	to be called as
6	介绍	jièshào	to introduce
7	来	lái	(used before a verb or a verbal expression, indicating an intended action)
8	吗	ma	(a particle used at the end of a question)
9	没关系	méi guānxi	it doesn't matter
10	名字	míngzi	name
11	嗯	ńg	eh (expressing question)
12	请问	qǐngwèn	may I ask…
	请	qǐng	please
	问	wèn	to ask
13	认识	rènshi	to know
14	什么	shénme	what
15	姓	xìng	to be surnamed
16	学生	xuéshēng	student
17	也	yě	too, also, as well
18	一下	yíxià	one time, once (used after a verb as its complement, indicating an act or an attempt)

UNIT 3

Wǒ cóng Yīngguó Lúndūn lái.
我从英国伦敦来。
I come from London, UK.

Objectives

In this unit, you'll learn:
- to ask someone's nationality and origin
- to introduce your nationality and origin

学习要点 | Key Points

Subject	Nationality and place of someone's origin
Goals	Learn to ask and introduce someone's nationality and origin
Grammar Points	• General questions with "吧" • Using "不" for negation • Special questions with "哪儿" or "什么地方" (both meaning "where")
Focal Sentences	Polite ways to make a request — 请再说一遍。
	Polite ways to ask questions — 请问，您是哪国人？
	Expressing thanks — 谢谢！
	Basic ways to ask and tell someone's nationality — A：你是哪国人？ B：我是日本人。
	Basic ways to ask and tell someone's origin — A：您是哪儿人？ B：我是北京人。 A：你是日本什么地方人？ B：我是日本东京人。
	Telling someone where you are from — 我从英国伦敦来。
Words and Phrases	从 来 姓名 国籍 再 说 一 遍 哪 国 人 哦 的 护照 给 谢谢 吧 不 爸爸 妈妈 地方 但 罗森 法国 美国 英国 日本 韩国 北京 上海 广东 东京 伦敦 中国
Chinese Characters	从 国 籍 再 说 遍 哪 人 哦 的 护 照 给 谢 吧 不 爸 妈 地 方 但 北 京 中

第 1 课 LESSON ONE

课文 | Text

海关。罗森正在过海关。
At the customs. Rawson is getting through the customs.

Hǎiguān gōngzuò rényuán **海关工作人员**	Nín hǎo! Xìngmíng? 您好！姓名？
Luó sēn **罗 森**	Duìbuqǐ, shénme? 对不起，什么？
Hǎiguān gōngzuò rényuán **海关工作人员**	Nín jiào shénme míngzi? 您叫什么名字？
Luó sēn **罗 森**	Luósēn. 罗森。
Hǎiguān gōngzuò rényuán **海关工作人员**	Guójí? 国籍？
Luó sēn **罗 森**	Qǐng zài shuō yí biàn. 请再说一遍。
Hǎiguān gōngzuò rényuán **海关工作人员**	Qǐngwèn, nín shì nǎ guó rén? 请问，您是哪国人？
Luó sēn **罗 森**	Fǎguó rén. 法国人。
Hǎiguān gōngzuò rényuán **海关工作人员**	Ò, Fǎguó rén. Nín de hùzhào? 哦，法国人。您的护照？
Luó sēn **罗 森**	Gěi nín. 给您。
Hǎiguān gōngzuò rényuán **海关工作人员**	Xièxie. 谢谢。

生词 | New Words 3-2

1	姓名	xìngmíng	名	name
2	国籍	guójí	名	nationality
3	再	zài	副	again, once more
4	说	shuō	动	to say, to speak
5	一	yī	数	one
6	遍	biàn	量	(measure word, mainly used for the times of actions)
7	哪	nǎ	代	which; where
8	国	guó	名	country, state
9	人	rén	名	people, person
10	哦	ò	叹	oh (expressing realization and understanding)
11	的	de	助	(used with an adjective or attribute phrase; indicating a possessive relationship)
12	护照	hùzhào	名	passport
13	给	gěi	动	to give
14	谢谢	xièxie	动	to thank

专有名词 | Proper Nouns

15	罗森	Luósēn		Rawson
16	法国	Fǎguó		France

第 2 课 LESSON TWO

课文 | Text

山口和子、玛丽和金太成在课间休息时聊天儿。 ▶3-3

Yamaguchi Kazuko, Mary and Kim Taesung are chatting during the class break.

Shānkǒu Hézǐ 山口和子	Nǐ hǎo, wǒ shì Shānkǒu Hézǐ. 你好，我是山口和子。
Mǎ lì 玛 丽	Nǐ hǎo, wǒ jiào Mǎlì. 你好，我叫玛丽。
Shānkǒu Hézǐ 山口和子	Nǐ shì Měiguó rén ma? 你是美国人吗？
Mǎ lì 玛 丽	Bù, wǒ shì Yīngguó rén. Nǐ shì nǎ guó rén? 不，我是英国人。你是哪国人？
Shānkǒu Hézǐ 山口和子	Wǒ shì Rìběn rén. 我是日本人。

金太成加入。

Kim Taesung joins in.

Jīn Tàichéng 金 太 成	Nǐmen hǎo! 你们好！
Mǎ lì 玛 丽	Nǐ hǎo, Jīn Tàichéng! Nǐ yě shì Rìběn rén ba? 你好，金太成！你也是日本人吧？
Jīn Tàichéng 金 太 成	Bù, wǒ bú shì Rìběn rén, wǒ shì Hánguó rén. 不，我不是日本人，我是韩国人。

生词 | New Words

| 1 | 吧 | ba | 语气 | a particle (used at the end of a question) |
| 2 | 不 | bù | 副 | no, not |

专有名词 | Proper Nouns

3	美国	Měiguó	United States of America (USA)
4	英国	Yīngguó	United Kingdom (UK)
5	日本	Rìběn	Japan
6	韩国	Hánguó	Republic of Korea

语法 | Grammar

1 带"吧"的一般疑问句
General questions with "吧"

"吧"用于一般疑问句句末,表示疑问。这样的问句往往不是单纯提问,而是包含了揣测的语气,表达了提问者的倾向,就像英语句末的"right"。

"吧" is used at the end of an interrogative sentence to show a sense of uncertainty. What this kind of sentences expresses is more like a speculation than a question. It is like the word "right" at the end of a sentence in English.

① Nǐ shì Rìběn rén ba?
你是日本人吧?
You are a Japanese, right?

② Nǐ yě cóng Yīngguó lái ba?
你也从英国来吧?
You also come from UK, right?

2 用"不"表达否定
Using "不" for negation

"不"用在动词、形容词或个别副词前,表示否定。

"不" is used before verbs, adjectives or particular adverbs to express negation.

1. Jīn Tàichéng bú shì Rìběn rén.
   金太成**不**是日本人。
   Kim Taesung is not a Japanese.

2. Tā māma bú shì Běijīng rén.
   他妈妈**不**是北京人。
   His mother is not a Beijinger.

第 3 课 LESSON THREE

课文 | Text

咖啡厅。李冬生和学生们在聊天儿。 ▶3-5

At a coffeehouse. Li Dongsheng and the students are chatting.

菲雅 (Fēiyǎ)
Lǎoshī, nín shì nǎr rén?
老师，您是哪儿人？

李冬生 (Lǐ Dōngshēng)
Wǒ shì Běijīng rén.
我是北京人。

山口和子 (Shānkǒu Hézǐ)
Nín bàba, māma yě shì Běijīng rén ma?
您爸爸、妈妈也是北京人吗？

李冬生 (Lǐ Dōngshēng)
Bù, wǒ bàba shì Shànghǎi rén, māma shì Guǎngdōng rén.
不，我爸爸是上海人，妈妈是广东人。

Shānkǒu, nǐ shì Rìběn shénme dìfang rén?
山口，你是日本什么地方人？

山口和子 (Shānkǒu Hézǐ)
Wǒ shì Rìběn Dōngjīng rén.
我是日本东京人。

李冬生 (Lǐ Dōngshēng)
Mǎlì, nǐ cóng shénme dìfang lái?
玛丽，你从什么地方来？

玛丽 (Mǎlì)
Wǒ cóng Yīngguó Lúndūn lái. Dàn wǒ māma bú shì Lúndūn rén. Wǒ māma de māma shì Zhōngguó rén.
我从英国伦敦来。但我妈妈不是伦敦人。我妈妈的妈妈是中国人。

李冬生 (Lǐ Dōngshēng)
Ó?
哦？

30 GREAT WALL CHINESE, A SIMPLE STEP TO SUCCESS!

生词 | New Words 🔊 3-6

1	爸爸	bàba	名	dad, father
2	妈妈	māma	名	mom, mother
3	地方	dìfang	名	place
4	从	cóng	介	from
5	来	lái	动	to come
6	但	dàn	连	but
7	哦	ó	叹	oh (expressing doubt)

专有名词 | Proper Nouns

8	北京	Běijīng	Beijing
9	上海	Shànghǎi	Shanghai
10	广东	Guǎngdōng	Guangdong
11	东京	Dōngjīng	Tokyo
12	伦敦	Lúndūn	London
13	中国	Zhōngguó	China

语法 | Grammar

3 用"哪儿"或"什么地方"的特殊疑问句
Special questions with "哪儿" or "什么地方" (both meaning "where")

用于询问地点。不能用肯定或否定回答，而要针对特定的疑问词，如"哪儿""什么地方""谁"等，作出回答。

It is used to inquire about a specific location and cannot be answered with affirmative or negative words. The answer should be specific to the question about "哪儿"(where), "什么地方"(where), "谁"(who), etc.

1. Lǐ lǎoshī shì nǎr rén?
   李老师是哪儿人？
   Where is Teacher Li from?

2. Nǐ shì shénme dìfang rén?
   你是什么地方人？
   Where are you from?

交际要点 | Communication Points

询问及回答籍贯的基本方式
Basic ways to ask and tell someone's origin

A: Nín shì nǎr rén?
   您是哪儿人？
   Where are you from?

B: Wǒ shì Běijīng rén.
   我是北京人。
   I'm from Beijing.

在口语中，用于询问他人的籍贯，一般说话人已经知道对方的国籍，想进一步了解更具体的信息，有时也可以用"您是什么地方人？"

In spoken language, it is used to ask someone's origin. The speaker generally already knows the person's nationality and wants to get more specific information. Sometimes, "您是什么地方人？" (literally: What place are you from?) is also used.

文化园 | Culture Corner

北京

北京是中国的首都，也是中国的政治、文化中心。北京有三千多年的历史，其中有800多年是都城，因此拥有非常多的帝王宫殿、园林和庙宇。北京的名胜古迹很多，如故宫、天坛、颐和园等。故宫是明清两代的皇家宫殿，历史上有24位皇帝在这儿居住过。天坛是皇帝祭天、祈谷的地方，其中的祈年殿是一座直径32米、高38米的圆形建筑，这么高大的建筑，竟然没有大梁，没有檩条，也没有铁钉，完全靠28根巨柱支撑。殿为圆形，象征天圆，瓦为蓝色，象征蓝天。是目前中国现存最大的皇家祭祀建筑群。颐和园是中国最后一个封建王朝——清朝时期的皇家园林，占地290万平方米，内有万寿山、昆明湖等著名景点，其中的仁寿殿是皇帝在此休养时办公的地方。还有长廊的上万幅绘画，没有一幅是相同的！如果你要去颐和园，请一定穿上舒适的鞋子，因为颐和园很大，可以逛的地方非常多。

Beijing

Beijing is the capital and also a political and cultural center of China. Beijing's history spans over three thousand years, including over 800 years as a capital. Because of this legacy, Beijing has an abundance of imperial palaces, gardens and temples. Beijing's many scenic spots of historical importance include the Forbidden City, the Temple of Heaven, and the Summer Palace, among many others. The Forbidden City is the palace where emperors of Ming Dynasty and Qing Dynasty resided, with a total of 24 emperors having called this palace home. At the Temple of Heaven emperors would worship heaven and pray for a plentiful harvest. It includes the Hall of Prayer for Good Harvests, a circular structure that is 32 meters in diameter and 38 meters tall. The Hall does not have any large roof beams, purlines or nails to support its weight, instead it is supported by 28 massive pillars, all made from exceptionally large trees. The round shape of the Hall symbolizes the cosmos, and its tiles symbolize the blue sky. Currently the Temple of Heaven is the largest architectural complex where the imperial family once offered sacrifices. The Summer Palace was an imperial garden of the final feudal dynasty of China, the Qing Dynasty. Encompassing 2.9 million square meters, the palace includes many famous scenic spots such as Longevity Hill and Kunming Lake. This Summer Palace also contains Renshou Hall (the Hall of Mercy and Longevity) where the emperor would work during his vacation time. Also found in this imperial garden is the "Covered Corridor" with over 10,000 paintings and no two the same! If you go to the Summer Palace, be sure to wear comfortable shoes, since it is very large and you'll have many places to explore.

生词复习 | Vocabulary Review

#			
1	爸爸	bàba	dad, father
2	吧	ba	a particle (used at the end of a question)
3	遍	biàn	(measure word, mainly used for the times of actions)
4	不	bù	no, not
5	从	cóng	from
6	但	dàn	but
7	的	de	(used with an adjective or attribute phrase; indicating a possessive relationship)
8	地方	dìfang	place
9	给	gěi	to give
10	国	guó	country, state
11	国籍	guójí	nationality
12	护照	hùzhào	passport
13	来	lái	to come
14	妈妈	māma	mom, mother
15	哪	nǎ	which; where
16	哦	ó	oh (expressing doubt)
17	哦	ò	oh (expressing realization and understanding)
18	人	rén	people, person
19	说	shuō	to say, to speak
20	谢谢	xièxie	to thank
21	姓名	xìngmíng	name
22	一	yī	one
23	再	zài	again, once more
24	北京	Běijīng	Beijing
25	东京	Dōngjīng	Tokyo
26	法国	Fǎguó	France
27	广东	Guǎngdōng	Guangdong
28	韩国	Hánguó	Republic of Korea
29	伦敦	Lúndūn	London
30	罗森	Luósēn	Rawson
31	美国	Měiguó	United States of America (USA)
32	日本	Rìběn	Japan
33	上海	Shànghǎi	Shanghai
34	英国	Yīngguó	United Kingdom (UK)
35	中国	Zhōngguó	China

UNIT 4

Wǒ zài yì jiā gōngsī gōngzuò.
我在一家公司工作。
I work for a company.

Objectives

In this unit, you'll learn:
- to ask someone's occupation
- to introduce your occupation

学习要点 | Key Points

Subject	Occupations
Goals	Learn to ask and introduce someone's occupation
Grammar Points	• Measure words "个", "名", "家" • Adverbials of place • Adverbials of time • Noun/pronoun+的+noun
Focal Sentences	Basic ways to ask and answer questions about someone's occupation — A：你做什么工作？ B：我是教练。
	Asking and telling where someone works — A：你在哪儿工作？ B：我在一家韩国公司工作。
	Affirming or negating questions or opinions of others — 对，我也工作。 不，我每天下午工作。
	Expressing one's likings — 我喜欢这个工作。 我喜欢画画。
Words and Phrases	家　公司　工作　大家　教练　护士　名　大学生　秘书　好　每天（每、天）图书馆　下午　在　哪儿　部门经理（部门、经理）　做　职员　记者　喜欢　这个　现在　画　啊　个　画家　珍妮　澳大利亚　德国
Chinese Characters	公　司　工　作　大　家　教　练　护　士　秘　书　每　天　图　书　馆　午　在　部　门　经　理　做　职　员　记　者　喜　欢　这　个　现　画　啊

第 1 课 LESSON ONE

课文 | Text

健身房内。麦克和学员们互相介绍自己的职业。 ▶4-1

In the gymnasium. Mike and the students are talking about their occupations.

Màikè 麦 克	Dàjiā hǎo! Wǒ shì jiàoliàn. Wǒ jiào Màikè, Wǒ shì Měiguó rén. 大家好！我是教练。我叫麦克，我是美国人。
Xuéyuán yī 学 员 1	Wǒ jiào Zhēnní, Àodàlìyà rén. Wǒ shì hùshi. 我叫珍妮，澳大利亚人。我是护士。
Xuéyuán èr 学 员 2	Wǒ xìng Lǐ, wǒ shì yì míng dàxuéshēng. Wǒ shì Zhōngguó rén. 我姓李，我是一名大学生。我是中国人。
Xuéyuán sān 学 员 3	Nǐmen hǎo! Wǒ shì Déguó rén. Wǒ zài yì jiā gōngsī gōngzuò, 你们好！我是德国人。我在一家公司工作， wǒ shì mìshū. 我是秘书。 ……
Màikè 麦 克	Hǎo, rènshi dàjiā hěn gāoxìng. 好，认识大家很高兴。Music!

音乐响起

Music starts

生词 | New Words ▶4-2

1	大家	dàjiā	代	everybody
2	教练	jiàoliàn	名	coach
3	护士	hùshi	名	nurse
4	名	míng	量	(measure word)
5	大学生	dàxuéshēng	名	college student
6	秘书	mìshū	名	secretary
7	好	hǎo	形	(used to express approval, conclusion, discontent, etc)

专有名词 | Proper Nouns

8	珍妮	Zhēnní		Jane
9	澳大利亚	Àodàlìyà		Australia
10	德国	Déguó		Germany

语法 | Grammar

1 量词"个""名""家"
Measure words "个","名","家"

　　量词表示事物（或动作）的数量单位，和前面的数词一起修饰名词。一个量词一般修饰特定的一些名词，要注意搭配。

　　Measure words are used in conjunction with a number to specify the quantity of an object (or action). They are used to modify nouns together with the preceding numerals. The measure word used depends on the following noun, so attention should be paid to the collocation.

1. Mǎlì shì yí gè huàjiā.
   玛丽是一**个**画家。
   Mary is a painter.

2. Wǒ shì yì míng dàxuéshēng.
   我是一**名**大学生。
   I am a college student.

3. Tā shì yì míng jìzhě.
   她是一**名**记者。
   She is a reporter.

4. Shānkǒu Hézǐ zài yì jiā Rìběn gōngsī gōngzuò.
   山口和子在一**家**日本公司工作。
   Yamaguchi Kazuko works for a Japanese company.

2 地点状语
Adverbials of place

　　状语是谓词性中心语前面的修饰语，常由副词充任。地点状语是表示地点的状语，如"在+处所名词"等。

　　Adverbs are the modifiers before predicative central words and are generally acted by adverbs. The adverbial of place is the adverbial modifier indicating a location, such as "在+noun" (representing location).

1. Nǐ zài nǎr gōngzuò?
   你**在哪儿**工作？
   Where do you work?

2. Wǒ zài yì jiā Hánguó gōngsī gōngzuò.
   我**在一家韩国公司**工作。
   I work for a Korean company.

第 2 课 LESSON TWO

课文 | Text

图书馆大厅。金太成和山口和子在聊天儿。 ▶4-3

At the lobby of the library. Kim Taesung and Yamaguchi Kazuko are chatting.

Shānkǒu Hézǐ 山口和子	Jīn Tàichéng, nǐ měi tiān lái túshūguǎn ma? 金太成，你每天来图书馆吗？
Jīn Tàichéng 金太成	Bù, wǒ měi tiān xiàwǔ gōngzuò. 不，我每天下午工作。
Shānkǒu Hézǐ 山口和子	Nǐ zài nǎr gōngzuò? 你在哪儿工作？
Jīn Tàichéng 金太成	Wǒ zài yì jiā Hánguó gōngsī gōngzuò, wǒ shì bùmén jīnglǐ. 我在一家韩国公司工作，我是部门经理。 Nǐ yě gōngzuò ma? 你也工作吗？
Shānkǒu Hézǐ 山口和子	Duì. Wǒ zài yì jiā Rìběn gōngsī gōngzuò. 对。我在一家日本公司工作。
Jīn Tàichéng 金太成	Nǐ zuò shénme gōngzuò? 你做什么工作？
Shānkǒu Hézǐ 山口和子	Wǒ shì gōngsī de zhíyuán. 我是公司的职员。

生词 | New Words ▶ 4-4

1	每天	měi tiān		everyday
	每	měi	代	every, each
	天	tiān	名	day
2	图书馆	túshūguǎn	名	library
3	下午	xiàwǔ	名	afternoon
4	工作	gōngzuò	动	to work
5	在	zài	介	at, in, on
6	哪儿	nǎr	代	where
7	家	jiā	量	(measure word)
8	公司	gōngsī	名	firm, company
9	部门经理	bùmén jīnglǐ		department manager
	部门	bùmén	名	department
	经理	jīnglǐ	名	manager
10	做	zuò	动	to do, to make
11	职员	zhíyuán	名	clerk

语法 | Grammar

3 时间状语
Adverbials of time

时间状语是谓词性中心语前面的表示时间的修饰语，常由副词充任，如"每天"等。

Adverbials of time are the modifiers before predicative central words representing time, and are generally acted by adverbs, such as "每天"(every day).

1. Nǐ měi tiān lái túshūguǎn ma?
   你**每天**来图书馆吗？
   Do you come to the library every day?

2. Wǒ měi tiān xiàwǔ gōngzuò.
   我**每天下午**工作。
   I work every afternoon.

3. Wǒ xiànzài bù gōngzuò.
   我**现在**不工作。
   I don't work now.

4 名词/代词+的+名词
Noun/pronoun+的+noun

名词或代词和"的"可以构成"的"字短语，修饰后面的名词，两个名词间常具有领属关系。

The first noun or pronoun and "的" together form a short phrase to modify the following noun; these two nouns generally have a relationship of belonging.

Wǒ shì gōngsī de zhíyuán.
我是**公司的职员**。
I am an employee of the company.

交际要点 | Communication Points

肯定/否定对方的询问或意见
Affirming or negating questions or opinions of others

1. Duì, wǒ yě gōngzuò.
   对，我也工作。
   Yes, I also work.

2. Bù, wǒ měi tiān xiàwǔ gōngzuò.
   不，我每天下午工作。
   No, I work every afternoon.

中国人在用"对""不"表示肯定和否定时，既可以判断事实，也可以判断对方的意思，二者在表达上略有不同。如，"你不是北京人吧？"如果被询问的人是北京人，他可以说"是，我是北京人"，也可以说"不，我是北京人"。前者用"是"判断事实，后者用"不"判断对方的意思。

The words "对"(yes/correct) and "不"(no) in Chinese both can express affirmation and negation. It is highly dependent on the proceeding statement or the fact. For example, when asked "你不是北京人吧？"(You aren't a Beijinger, right?), if the person happens to be from Beijing, he can say "是, 我是北京人"(Yes, I am a Beijinger), which affirms the fact; he can also say "不, 我是北京人"(No, I am a Beijinger), which negates the proceeding statement.

第 3 课 LESSON THREE

课文 | Text

公寓阳台。玛丽和菲雅在谈职业。 ▶4-5

At the apartment's balcony. Mary and Faye are talking about occupations.

Mǎ lì	Fēiyǎ, nǐ zuò shénme gōngzuò?	
玛丽	菲雅，你做什么工作？	
Fēi yǎ	Wǒ shì yì míng jìzhě.	
菲雅	我是一名记者。	
Mǎ lì	Nǐ xǐhuan zhège gōngzuò ma?	
玛丽	你喜欢这个工作吗？	
Fēi yǎ	Wǒ hěn xǐhuan. Mǎlì, nǐ gōngzuò ma?	
菲雅	我很喜欢。玛丽，你工作吗？	
Mǎ lì	Wǒ xiànzài bù gōngzuò.	
玛丽	我现在不工作。	
Fēi yǎ	Nǐ xǐhuan zuò shénme?	
菲雅	你喜欢做什么？	
Mǎ lì	Wǒ xǐhuan huà huà.	
玛丽	我喜欢画画。	
Fēi yǎ	À, nǐ shì yí gè huàjiā!	
菲雅	啊，你是一个画家！	

生词 | New Words 🔊 4-6

1	记者	jìzhě	名	reporter
2	喜欢	xǐhuan	动	to like
3	这个	zhège	代	this one
4	现在	xiànzài	名	now
5	画	huà	动/名	to paint, to draw; painting, drawing
6	啊	à	叹	aha (used to express sudden realization)
7	个	gè	量	(measure word)
8	画家	huàjiā	名	painter, artist

文化园 | Culture Corner

Shanghai

In most cases, a nation's capital is its largest city. Is this the case in China? In terms of both spatial area and population, Shanghai is China's largest city. From north to south, Shanghai spans about 120 kilometers, while from east to west the city extends about 100 kilometers. A city of such size means that no matter how you travel in Shanghai, even having a cursory look of the city will require a lot of time! According to the statistics in 2019, Beijing's permanent population is approximately 21.5 million, which is surpassed by the 24.2 million of Shanghai. Despite such an enormous population, Shanghai's transportation system, shopping opportunities and entertainment options are all very convenient. Shanghai has a well-developed public transportation network, with well-designed subway lines and high operation efficiency. Convenience stores are widely distributed and the "small but beautiful" mode improves shopping efficiency. Shanghai's infrastructure is also very unique. On the Bund, there are city's architectural treasures like the Tower of Asia (built in 1916), the Shanghai Society Tower (start using in 1910). The city's famous Customs Building (rebuilt in 1925) and other dozens of unique buildings are also on the Bund. A trip to Shanghai must include an exploration of these famous buildings. We hope that you will get a chance to visit them someday!

上海

一般情况下，首都应该是一个国家最大的城市，那中国呢？从面积、人口等综合来看，上海是最大的城市。上海市南北长约120公里，东西宽约100公里，不管是从南到北，还是从东到西，即使是走马观花，也需要很多时间！根据2019年的数据统计，北京的常住人口大概2,150万，上海大概2,420万。虽然有这么多人，但出行、购物、游玩等方面还是很便利的。上海的公共交通发达完善，地铁线路设计合理，运营效率很高。便利店分布范围广，小而美的模式提高了购物效率。上海的城市建设也非常有特色，在最有名的上海"外滩"，有建于1916年的亚细亚大楼，启用于1910年的上海总会大楼，重建于1925年的海关大楼等，数十栋建筑风格迥异，是游上海的必去之地，你也一定要去啊！

生词复习 | Vocabulary Review

#	汉字	Pinyin	English
1	啊	à	aha (used to express sudden realization)
2	部门经理	bùmén jīnglǐ	department manager
	部门	bùmén	department
	经理	jīnglǐ	manager
3	大家	dàjiā	everybody
4	大学生	dàxuéshēng	college student
5	个	gè	(measure word)
6	工作	gōngzuò	to work
7	公司	gōngsī	firm, company
8	好	hǎo	(used to express approval, conclusion, discontent, etc)
9	护士	hùshi	nurse
10	画	huà	to paint, to draw; painting, drawing
11	画家	huàjiā	painter, artist
12	记者	jìzhě	reporter
13	家	jiā	(measure word)
14	教练	jiàoliàn	coach
15	每天	měi tiān	every day
	每	měi	every, each
	天	tiān	day
16	秘书	mìshū	secretary
17	名	míng	(measure word)
18	哪儿	nǎr	where
19	图书馆	túshūguǎn	library
20	喜欢	xǐhuan	to like
21	下午	xiàwǔ	afternoon
22	现在	xiànzài	now
23	在	zài	at, in, on
24	这个	zhège	this one
25	职员	zhíyuán	clerk
26	做	zuò	to do, to make
27	澳大利亚	Àodàlìyà	Australia
28	德国	Déguó	Germany
29	珍妮	Zhēnní	Jane

UNIT 5

Nǐ jīnnián duō dà?
你今年多大?
How old are you?

Objectives

In this unit, you'll learn:
- to ask someone's age
- to tell someone your age

学习要点 | Key Points

Subject	Age
Goals	Learn to ask and tell someone's age
Grammar Points	• Special questions with "几" (indicating quantity) • Noun-predicate sentences • The use of numerals • Reduplication of verbs
Focal Sentences	Asking a child's age — A：你今年几岁（了）？ B：我四岁（了）。
	Asking an adult's age — A：你今年多大（了）？ B：我 21 岁。
	Asking a senior's age — A：您今年多大年纪（了）？ B：我 65 岁了。
	Making suggestions or inquiring about someone's opinion — 你星期六上午来，可以吗？/ 好吗？
	Identifying someone — A：您认识这个人吗？ B：我（不）认识这个人。
Words and Phrases	今年　多大（多、大）　小朋友　几　岁　猜　对　阿姨 这　秘密　事　想　健身　女　星期六　上午　可以 大妈　京剧　声音　真　好听　年纪　外婆　看　李明
Chinese Characters	今　年　多　小　朋　友　几　岁　猜　对　阿　姨　秘 密　事　想　健　身　女　星　期　六　上　可　以　剧 声　音　真　听　纪　外　婆　看

48　GREAT WALL CHINESE, A SIMPLE STEP TO SUCCESS!

第 1 课 LESSON ONE

课文 | Text

玛丽看见一个小男孩。 5-1
Mary sees a little boy.

Mǎ lì		Nǐ hǎo, xiǎopéngyǒu! Nǐ jiào shénme míngzi?
玛 丽		你好，小朋友！你叫什么名字？
Xiǎo nánhái		Wǒ jiào Lǐ Míng.
小男孩		我叫李明。
Mǎ lì		Nǐ jīnnián jǐ suì?
玛 丽		你今年几岁？
Xiǎo nánhái		Nǐ cāi wǒ jǐ suì?
小男孩		你猜我几岁？
Mǎ lì		Wǔ suì?
玛 丽		5岁？
Xiǎo nánhái		Bú duì.
小男孩		不对。
Mǎ lì		Qī suì?
玛 丽		7岁？
Xiǎo nánhái		Bú duì, wǒ jīnnián liù suì. Āyí, nǐ duō dà?
小男孩		不对，我今年6岁。阿姨，你多大？
Mǎ lì		Zhè shì gè mìmì.
玛 丽		这是个秘密。

生词 | New Words 5-2

1	小朋友	xiǎopéngyǒu	名	little friend
2	几	jǐ	代	how many; several
3	岁	suì	量	(measure word, used for age)
4	猜	cāi	动	to guess
5	对	duì	形	correct, right
6	阿姨	āyí	名	aunty
7	多大	duō dà		how old
	多	duō	代	how
	大	dà	形	old; big
8	这	zhè	代	this
9	秘密	mìmì	名	secret

专有名词 | Proper Nouns

10	李明	Lǐ Míng		Li Ming

语法 | Grammar

1 用"几"的特殊疑问句
Special questions with "几" (indicating quantity)

"几"一般用于询问或表示不超过十的数量，也可以用在"十""百""千""万""亿"等之前和"十"之后，表示不确定的数量。

"几" is usually used to ask about or refer to numbers less than 10. It can also be used before "十"(ten), "百"(hundred), "千"(thousand), "万"(ten thousand) and "亿"(hundred million) or after "十"(ten) to refer to an uncertain number more than 10 and less than 20.

1 Nǐ jīnnián jǐ suì le?
你今年几岁了？
How old are you?

2 Wǒ lái Běijīng jǐshí nián le.
我来北京几十年了。
I've come to Beijing for several decades.

3 Zhège háizi zhǐyǒu shíjǐ suì.
这个孩子只有十几岁。
This child is only over ten years old.

2 名词谓语句
Noun-predicate sentences

谓语一般由动词和形容词性词语/短语充任，但在汉语中，名词/名词性短语在一定条件下也可以充任谓语，这类谓语一般只限于说明时间、天气、价格、年龄、籍贯和容貌等。

Verbs and adjectival words/phrases generally act as predicates, while in Chinese, under certain conditions, nominal words/phrases can also act as predicates, and such kinds of predicates are limited to describing time, weather, price, age, place of origin, appearance, etc.

1 Wǒ jīnnián liù suì.
我今年6岁。
I am 6 years old.

2 Tā jīnnián liùshíwǔ suì.
她今年65岁。
She's 65 years old.

第 2 课　LESSON TWO

课文 | Text

健身房。麦克正在指导学员健身，张圆圆走进来要报名。 ▶5-3

At the gymnasium. Mike is coaching the students on how to do an aerobic exercise when Zhang Yuanyuan comes in to sign up for aerobics.

Mài kè 麦 克	Yī, èr, sān, sì, wǔ, liù, qī, bā; èr, èr, sān, sì… 1、2、3、4、5、6、7、8；2、2、3、4……
Zhāng Yuányuan 张 圆 圆	Jiàoliàn, nǐ hǎo! 教练，你好！
Mài kè 麦 克	Nǐ hǎo! Shénme shì? 你好！什么事？
Zhāng Yuányuan 张 圆 圆	Wǒ xiǎng jiànshēn. 我想 健身。
Mài kè 麦 克	Nǐ jiào shénme míngzi? Jīnnián duō dà? 你叫什么名字？今年多大？
Zhāng Yuányuan 张 圆 圆	Wǒ jiào Zhāng Yuányuan, èrshíyī suì. 我叫张 圆圆，21岁。
Mài kè 麦 克	Zhāng Yuányuan, nǚ, èrshíyī suì. Hǎo, nǐ Xīngqīliù shàngwǔ lái, kěyǐ ma? 张 圆圆，女，21岁。好，你星期六上午来，可以吗？
Zhāng Yuányuan 张 圆 圆	Kěyǐ! 可以！

生词 | New Words 🔊 5-4

1	事	shì	名	business, matter
2	想	xiǎng	动	to want
3	健身	jiànshēn	动	to keep fit
4	今年	jīnnián	名	this year
5	女	nǚ	形	female
6	星期六	Xīngqīliù	名	Saturday
7	上午	shàngwǔ	名	morning, am
8	可以	kěyǐ	动	can, may

语法 | Grammar

3 数词的用法
The use of numerals

　　数词是表示数目的词，包括基数词和序数词。基数词可以单用，也可以和量词一起构成数量短语，修饰名词。

　　Numerals are the words that express numbers, including cardinal numerals and ordinal numerals. Cardinal numerals can either be used alone or together with measure words to compose a quantitative phrase and modify nouns.

yī　èr　sān　sì　wǔ　liù　qī　bā　　èrshíyī　　liùshíwǔ　　bāshísān
1　2　3　4　5　6　7　8　　21　　65　　83

shí gè rén　　sān jiān fángjiān
10 个人　　3 间房间

第 3 课 LESSON THREE

课文 | Text

玛丽在四合院外看老人们练唱京剧。 5-5

Mary is watching some seniors practising Peking opera outside a Siheyuan.

Mǎlì	Dàmā, zhè shì jīngjù ba?	
玛丽	大妈，这是京剧吧？	
Lǎorén yī	Duì.	
老人1	对。	
Mǎlì	Nín de shēngyīn zhēn hǎotīng! Nín jīnnián duō dà niánjì?	
玛丽	您的声音真好听！您今年多大年纪？	
Lǎorén yī	Wǒ jīnnián liùshíwǔ suì. Nǐ shì……?	
老人1	我今年65岁。你是……？	
Mǎlì	Wǒ jiào Mǎlì, cóng Yīngguó lái. Nín rènshi zhège rén ma?	
玛丽	我叫玛丽，从英国来。您认识这个人吗？	
Lǎorén yī	Tā shì shéi?	
老人1	她是谁？	
Mǎlì	Tā shì wǒ māma de māma.	
玛丽	她是我妈妈的妈妈。	
Lǎorén yī	Ò, nǐ wàipó. Tā jīnnián duō dà niánjì?	
老人1	哦，你外婆。她今年多大年纪？	
Mǎlì	Bāshísān suì.	
玛丽	83岁。	
Lǎorén yī	Bāshísān suì…… Nǐmen lái kànkan, rènshi zhège rén ma?	
老人1	83岁……你们来看看，认识这个人吗？	
Zhòng lǎorén	Bú rènshi, bú rènshi.	
众老人	不认识，不认识。	
Zhào Yùlán	Wǒ kànkan.……	
赵玉兰	我看看。……	

GREAT WALL CHINESE, A SIMPLE STEP TO SUCCESS!

生词 | New Words 🔊 5-6

1	大妈	dàmā	名	aunt
2	京剧	jīngjù	名	Peking opera
3	声音	shēngyīn	名	voice
4	真	zhēn	副	really
5	好听	hǎotīng	形	pleasant to hear, sound nice
6	年纪	niánjì	名	age
7	外婆	wàipó	名	grandmother
8	看	kàn	动	to take a look

语法 | Grammar

4 动词重叠
Reduplication of verbs

多数动作动词都可以重叠，重叠后表示动作持续或重复，有短时、量小或尝试等意味。

Most of the action verbs can be reduplicated to express the continuation and repetition of the action and imply a short time, small quantity, or an attempt, etc.

1 Nǐmen lái kànkan.
你们来看看。
Come and take a look.

2 Dàjiā lái rènshi rènshi.
大家来认识认识。
Let's get to know each other.

交际要点 | Communication Points

1 询问孩子的年龄
Asking a child's age

A: Nǐ jīnnián jǐ suì le?
你今年几岁(了)?
How old are you?

B: Wǒ jīnnián liù suì.
我今年六岁。
I'm six years old.

2 询问成年人的年龄
Asking an adult's age

A: Nǐ jīnnián duō dà le?
你今年多大(了)?
How old are you?

B: Wǒ jīnnián èrshíyī suì.
我今年 21 岁。
I'm 21 years old.

3 询问老年人的年龄
Asking a senior's age

A: Nín jīnnián duō dà niánjì le?
您今年多大年纪(了)?
How old are you?

B: Wǒ jīnnián liùshíwǔ suì.
我今年 65 岁。
I'm 65 years old.

汉语中询问年龄一共有三种常用的方式:"几岁",用于询问儿童的年龄;"多大",用于询问成年人的年龄;"多大年纪",用于询问老年人的年龄。三种询问方式的回答都是"主语+数词+岁(了)"。

In Chinese, there are three commonly used ways to ask someone's age: "几岁" to ask a child's age, "多大" to ask an adult's age, and "多大年纪" to ask a senior's age. The response to these three questions is "subject+number+岁(years old)".

文化园 | Culture Corner

年龄

同一年出生的人中，有些中国人报出的年龄可能比外国人多一岁，这是因为中国人的年龄有周岁和虚岁之说。周岁就是实际出生的年月，虚岁则是在周岁的基础上加一岁。为什么呢？因为有的中国人会把在妈妈肚子里生长的10个月也算进去。这是很有道理的，因为在我们看到这个世界以前，其实就已经作为一个生命体存在了。

那么，中国人在年龄问题上，有些什么样的要求呢？中国从1986年开始实行九年义务制教育，一般要求小孩子从6周岁开始，要接受6年的小学教育和3年的初中教育。中国"婚姻法"规定：男性满22周岁、女性满20周岁才能结婚。中国人什么时候退休呢？不同的行业和工作有不同的规定，一般是男性60岁、女性55岁，当然也得是"周岁"了。

Age

Some Chinese people are likely to state their age as exactly one year older than a non-Chinese individual born in the same year. This is because the Chinese consider age in terms of two systems of "周岁"(zhōusuì) and "虚岁"(xūsuì). "周岁" is the specific age of a person based on the year, month and day of his/her birth, while the "虚岁" system considers an individual already one year old at birth. Why are there two age systems? Some Chinese people claim that it is because age should factor in the ten months or so spent developing inside the womb, since at that time the baby is already a life form.

What sort of age-related rules exist in China? Since 1986 China has had a system of nine-year compulsory education, requiring that children begin school when they are six years old (according to the "周岁" system). All children must then go through six years of elementary school and three years of middle school, but high school is not mandatory. Chinese marriage law specifies that males must be 22 years old and females 20 years old in order to marry legally. At what age do Chinese people retire? Different industries and jobs have different regulations, and generally men are allowed to retire at the age of 60 and women at the age of 55. Of course, these marriage and retirement regulations are also based on the "周岁" system.

生词复习 | Vocabulary Review

1	阿姨	āyí	aunty	13	秘密	mìmì	secret
2	猜	cāi	to guess	14	年纪	niánjì	age
3	大妈	dàmā	aunt	15	女	nǚ	female
4	对	duì	correct, right	16	上午	shàngwǔ	morning, am
5	多大	duō dà	how old	17	声音	shēngyīn	voice
	多	duō	how	18	事	shì	business, matter
	大	dà	old; big	19	岁	suì	(measure word, used for age)
6	好听	hǎotīng	pleasant to hear, sound nice				
				20	外婆	wàipó	grandmother
7	几	jǐ	how many; several	21	想	xiǎng	to want
8	健身	jiànshēn	to keep fit	22	小朋友	xiǎopéngyǒu	little friend
9	今年	jīnnián	this year	23	星期六	Xīngqīliù	Saturday
10	京剧	jīngjù	Peking opera	24	这	zhè	this
11	看	kàn	to take a look	25	真	zhēn	really
12	可以	kěyǐ	can, may	26	李明	Lǐ Míng	Li Ming

UNIT 6

Tā de nán péngyou hěn shuài!
她的男朋友很帅!
Her boyfriend is very handsome!

Objectives

In this unit, you'll learn:
- to use simple words to describe someone's height and weight
- to describe someone's general appearance

Great Wall Chinese

学习要点 | Key Points

Subject	One's figure and features
Goals	Learn to use simple words to describe someone's height, weight and general appearance
Grammar points	• Alternative questions • Questions with "多+adjective" • Affirmative-negative questions • Sentences with adjectival predicates and adverbs of degree
Focal sentences	Talking about someone's appearance — A：他帅不帅？ B：他很帅。 Asking someone's wishes: 想+verb phrase+吗？ — 你想找这样的男朋友吗？ Talking about someone's height and weight — 她1米65。 我体重54公斤。
Words and phrases	男朋友 帅 怎么样 不错 外国人（外国） 大学 学习 男 还是 个子 高 米 左右 找 这样 小姐 累 明天 休息 要 太 胖 啊 体重 公斤 还 可以 那时 漂亮 外公 汉语
Chinese characters	男 帅 怎 样 错 习 还 子 米 左 右 找 样 姐 累 明 天 休 息 要 太 胖 体 重 公 斤 那 时 漂 亮 汉 语

第 1 课 LESSON ONE

课文 | Text

咖啡厅。张芳芳和张圆圆在谈论健身教练。

At the coffeehouse. Zhang Fangfang and Zhang Yuanyuan are talking about the coach in the gymnasium.

Zhāng Fāngfāng / 张芳芳: Nǐ de jiànshēn jiàoliàn zěnmeyàng? / 你的健身教练怎么样？

Zhāng Yuányuan / 张圆圆: Búcuò. Tā shì yí gè wàiguó rén, zà yí gè dàxué xuéxí Hànyǔ. / 不错。他是一个外国人，在一个大学学习汉语。

Zhāng Fāngfāng / 张芳芳: Wàiguó rén? Nán de háishi nǚ de? / 外国人？男的还是女的？

Zhāng Yuányuan / 张圆圆: Nán de, gèzi hěn gāo. / 男的，个子很高。

Zhāng Fāngfāng / 张芳芳: Tā duō gāo? / 他多高？

Zhāng Yuányuan / 张圆圆: Yì mǐ bā líng zuǒyòu. / 1米80左右。

Zhāng Fāngfāng / 张芳芳: Shuài bú shuài? / 帅不帅？

Zhāng Yuányuan / 张圆圆: Hěn shuài. / 很帅。

Zhāng Fāngfāng / 张芳芳: Nǐ xiǎng zhǎo zhèyàng de nán péngyou ma? / 你想找这样的男朋友吗？

Zhāng Yuányuan / 张圆圆: Shénme? / 什么？

生词 | New Words 6-2

1	怎么样	zěnmeyàng	代	how
2	不错	búcuò	形	not bad
3	外国人	wàiguó rén		foreigner
	外国	wàiguó	名	foreign country
4	大学	dàxué	名	university
5	学习	xuéxí	动	to learn
6	男	nán	形	male
7	还是	háishi	副	or
8	个子	gèzi	名	stature, height
9	高	gāo	形	tall
10	米	mǐ	量	meter (measure word)
11	左右	zuǒyòu	名	about, or so (used after a number)
12	帅	shuài	形	handsome
13	找	zhǎo	动	to look for
14	这样	zhèyàng	代	such, like this
15	男朋友	nán péngyou		boyfriend

专有名词 | Proper Nouns

16	汉语	Hànyǔ		Chinese language

语法 | Grammar

1 选择疑问句
Alternative questions

选择疑问句表示疑问，提问者提供两个或两个以上的选择，回答一般要从中选一。

An alternative question is used when asking someone to make a choice. This kind of questions allow the questioner to list two or more choices for the person questioned. The later one needs to choose one from the choices.

1 Nǐ de jiàoliàn shì nán de háishi nǚ de?
你的教练是男的还是女的？
Is your coach a man or woman?

2 Luósēn shì Fǎguó rén háishi Yīngguó rén?
罗森是法国人还是英国人？
Is Rawson a French or British?

2 带"多+形容词"的疑问句
Questions with "多+adjective"

"多"用在疑问句中，询问程度和数量，后面的形容词一般是单音节词。

"多" in interrogative sentences is used to ask about degree and quantity, and the adjective following it is generally monosyllabic.

1 Nǐ duō gāo?
你多高？
How tall are you?

2 Nǐ duō dà le?
你多大（了）？
How old are you?

3 Nín duō dà niánjì le?
您多大年纪（了）？
How old are you?

交际要点 | Communication Points

询问某人身高
Asking about someone's height

1 Tā duō gāo?
他多高？
How tall is he?

2 Tā yì mǐ bā líng zuǒyòu.
他1米80左右。
He is about 1.80 meters tall.

"多+形容词"的结构用于询问程度。"多高"用于询问他人身高，如"他多高？""他1米85"。注意答句的正确读法是"Tā yì mǐ bā wǔ"。

The structure of "多+adjective" is used to ask degree. "多高" (How tall) is used to ask people their height. For example, for the question "他多高？"(How tall is he?), an appropriate response would be "Tā yì mǐ bā wǔ" (He is 1.85 meters tall).

第 2 课 LESSON TWO

课文 | Text

张圆圆在健身房锻炼，麦克走了过来。 ▶6-3

Zhang Yuanyuan is doing exercises in the gymnasium when Mike comes over.

Mài kè	Zhāng xiǎojiě, lèi bú lèi?	
麦 克	张 小姐，累不累？	
Zhāng Yuányuan	Bú lèi.	
张 圆 圆	不累。	
Mài kè	Míngtiān nǐ xiūxi yíxià ba.	
麦 克	明天你休息一下吧。	
Zhāng Yuányuan	Bù, wǒ yào lái, wǒ tài pàng le!	
张 圆 圆	不，我要来，我太胖了！	
Mài kè	Nǐ bú pàng a!	
麦 克	你不胖啊！	
Zhāng Yuányuan	Wǒ tǐzhòng wǔshísì gōngjīn.	
张 圆 圆	我体重 54 公斤。	
Mài kè	Hái kěyǐ. Nǐ duō gāo?	
麦 克	还可以。你多高？	
Zhāng Yuányuan	Yì mǐ liù wǔ.	
张 圆 圆	1 米 65。	
Mài kè	Yì mǐ liù wǔ, wǔshísì gōngjīn, bú pàng.	
麦 克	1 米 65，54 公斤，不胖。	

生词 | New Words 6-4

1	小姐	xiǎojiě	名	miss
2	累	lèi	形	tired, fatigued
3	明天	míngtiān	名	tomorrow
4	休息	xiūxi	动	to have a rest
5	要	yào	动	to want (to do)
6	太	tài	副	too
7	胖	pàng	形	overweight
8	啊	a	语气	ah (modal particle)
9	体重	tǐzhòng	名	weight
10	公斤	gōngjīn	量	kilogram (measure word)
11	还	hái	副	yet, still
12	可以	kěyǐ	形	passable, not bad

语法 | Grammar

3 正反疑问句
Affirmative-negative questions

正反问句表示疑问，由谓语的肯定形式和否定形式并列组成，回答时要从中选择其一。

It is used in questions and is composed of affirmative and negative forms of predicates, one of which is the answer.

1 Nǐ lèi bú lèi?
你累不累？
Are you tired (or not)?

2 Nǐ xǐhuan bù xǐhuan?
你喜欢不喜欢？
Do you like it (or not)?

4 形容词谓语句及程度副词
Sentences with adjectival predicates and adverbs of degree

形容词单独做谓语，表示事物性状的变化和发展，或带有比较、对照的意味。副词是具有修饰动词、形容词或整个句子功能的虚词。程度副词是表示程度的副词，可以用在形容词谓语之前，如"很""非常""太""真"等。

Adjectives as predicates indicate changes or development of properties of things, or indicate comparison and contrast. Adverbs are words which can modify verbs, adjectives or full sentences. Adverbs of degree denote the degree of the adjectives, such as "很"(very), "非常"(extremely), "太"(too), "真"(truly), usually used before predicates of adjective.

1 Wǒ de jiàoliàn hěn shuài.
我的教练很帅。
My coach is very handsome.

2 Tā tài pàng le!
他太胖了！
He's truely overweight!

2 Mǎlì de wàipó zhēn piàoliang!
玛丽的外婆真漂亮！
Mary's grandmother is really beautiful!

第 3 课 LESSON THREE

课文 | Text

公寓阳台。玛丽拿着照片向菲雅介绍自己的外婆。 ▶6-5

At the apartment's balcony. Mary is showing Faye a picture and telling Faye about her grandmother.

Fēi yǎ 菲 雅	Tā shì shéi? 她是谁？	
Mǎ lì 玛 丽	Tā shì wǒ wàipó, tā nàshí shíbā suì. 她是我外婆，她那时 18 岁。	
Fēi yǎ 菲 雅	Tā zhēn piàoliang! Tā shì Zhōngguó rén ba? 她真漂亮！她是 中国 人吧？	
Mǎ lì 玛 丽	Duì, tā shì Běijīng rén. 对，她是北京人。	
Fēi yǎ 菲 雅	Nà nǐ wàigōng ne? 那你外公呢？	
Mǎ lì 玛 丽	Wǒ wàigōng shì Yīngguó rén. 我外公是英国人。	
Fēi yǎ 菲 雅	Ō. 噢。	

生词 | New Words ▶6-6

1	那时	nàshí	代	then, at that time
2	漂亮	piàoliang	形	pretty
3	外公	wàigōng	名	grandfather

文化园 | Culture Corner

长江

The Yangtze River

China's Yangtze River (长江, Chángjiāng) is the longest river not only in China, but also in Asia. How long is it exactly? In total it is over 6,300 kilometers in length. Where might be the source of such a long river? It is the Tanggula Mountains in western China. Where does the Yangtze River flow through? Its artery passes through 11 different Chinese provinces and autonomous regions before spilling into the Donghai Sea in Shanghai. Along the banks of the Yangtze River there are scores of cities of all sizes, such as Chongqing, the "mountain city", which is described as "a city built on top of mountains, with mountains immersed therein". Another city on the Yangtze River's bank is Wuhan, which is of about 8,500 square kilometers and even larger than Shanghai. Part of the reason for Wuhan's enormous size is a river, the Hanjiang River (汉江, Hànjiāng) that crosses the city. The river divides the city into three large districts respectively named the "Wuchang", "Hankou" and "Hanyang". Of course, the most satisfying way to experience the Yangtze River is to take a cruise from Chongqing to Yichang. Along this journey you will enjoy seeing the Three Gorges Dam and many sites of great historic importance and natural beauty, but first you must manage to secure a ticket!

中国有一条河，叫"长江"，是中国最长的河，也是亚洲第一长河。长江有多长呢？全长6,300多公里。这么长的一条大河，是从什么地方流出来的呢？是从中国西部的唐古拉山脉。流到哪里去了？它的干流流经了中国11个省市自治区，最后从上海注入东海。长江两岸有几十个大大小小的城市，如"山城"重庆，它的特点是"城在山上，山在城中"；如武汉，有8,500平方公里左右，比上海的面积还大，因为有一条横贯市区的"汉江"，把武汉一分为三，形成武昌、汉口、汉阳三个城区。当然，最惬意的是坐上游轮，从重庆出发到宜昌，沿途能看到长江上著名的"三峡大坝"以及无数个历史悠久、风光秀美的景点。不过你要记得先预订船票！

生词复习 | Vocabulary Review

#			
1	啊	a	ah (modal particle)
2	不错	búcuò	not bad
3	大学	dàxué	university
4	高	gāo	tall
5	个子	gèzi	stature, height
6	公斤	gōngjīn	kilogram (measure word)
7	还	hái	yet, still
8	还是	háishi	or
9	可以	kěyǐ	passable, not bad
10	累	lèi	tired, fatigued
11	米	mǐ	meter (measure word)
12	明天	míngtiān	tomorrow
13	那时	nàshí	then, at that time
14	男	nán	male
15	男朋友	nán péngyou	boyfriend
16	胖	pàng	overweight
17	漂亮	piàoliang	pretty
18	帅	shuài	handsome
19	太	tài	too
20	体重	tǐzhòng	weight
21	外公	wàigōng	grandfather
22	外国人	wàiguó rén	foreigner
	外国	wàiguó	foreign country
23	小姐	xiǎojiě	miss
24	休息	xiūxi	to have a rest
25	学习	xuéxí	to learn
26	要	yào	to want (to do)
27	怎么样	zěnmeyàng	how
28	找	zhǎo	to look for
29	这样	zhèyàng	such, like this
30	左右	zuǒyòu	about, or so (used after a number)
31	汉语	Hànyǔ	Chinese language

UNIT 7

Wǒ zhù zài Yángguāng Xiǎoqū.
我住在阳光小区。
I live in Yangguang Residential Neighborhood.

Objectives

In this unit, you'll learn:
- to tell location
- to tell address

Great Wall Chinese

学习要点 | Key Points

Subject	Address
Goals	Learn to tell location and address
Grammar Points	• The use of ordinal numbers • The expression of direction and position • The structure of "A+离+B+远/近"
Focal Sentences	Asking or telling someone's address A：你住在哪儿？ B：我住在阳光小区 24 号楼 17 层 1708 号。
	Bidding farewell 明天见。 一会儿见。
	Asking or telling a distance A：第二医院离这儿远不远？ B：不太远。
	Responding to thanks 别客气。
Words and Phrases	住 我们 学校 有 健美操 比赛 参加 当 去 宿舍 号 楼 房间 电话 见 喂 家 里 今天 晚上 宴会 饭店 接 小区 层 前边 等 一会儿 第二（第、二） 医院 路 离 这儿 远 知道 东边 别客气（别、客气） 阳光小区 长安饭店 第二医院 东城路
Chinese Characters	住 校 有 美 操 比 赛 参 加 当 去 宿 舍 号 楼 房 间 电 话 见 喂 里 晚 宴 会 饭 店 接 区 层 前 边 等 医 院 路 离 远 知 道 东 别 客 气

第 1 课 LESSON ONE

课文 | Text

健身房内。张圆圆请麦克去她所在的学校当健身教练。 7-1

In the gymnasium. Zhang Yuanyuan asks Mike to work as a callisthenics coach at her university.

张圆圆 Jiàoliàn, wǒmen xuéxiào yǒu gè jiànměicāo bǐsài.
教练，我们学校有个健美操比赛。

麦克 Shì ma? Nǐ cānjiā ma?
是吗？你参加吗？

张圆圆 Wǒ cānjiā. Nǐ dāng wǒmen de jiàoliàn, hǎo ma?
我参加。你当我们的教练，好吗？

麦克 Hǎo a! Wǒ yě xiǎng qù nǐmen xuéxiào kànkan.
好啊！我也想去你们学校看看。

张圆圆 Nǐ míngtiān qù, kěyǐ ma?
你明天去，可以吗？

麦克 Kěyǐ. Wǒ qù zhǎo nǐ ba. Nǐ zhù zài nǎr?
可以。我去找你吧。你住在哪儿？

张圆圆 Wǒ zhù zài xuéshēng sùshè sān hào lóu sān líng èr hào fángjiān,
我住在学生宿舍3号楼 302号房间，
diànhuà shì bā èr yāo jiǔ sì liù qī wǔ.
电话是82194675。

麦克 Hǎo, míngtiān jiàn.
好，明天见。

生词 | New Words 🔊 7-2

1	我们	wǒmen	代	we, us
2	学校	xuéxiào	名	school; university
3	有	yǒu	动	there be; to have
4	健美操	jiànměicāo	名	callisthenics
5	比赛	bǐsài	名	competition
6	参加	cānjiā	动	to participate in
7	当	dāng	动	to act as, to serve as
8	去	qù	动	to go to
9	住	zhù	动	to live
10	宿舍	sùshè	名	dormitory
11	号	hào	量	number, order
12	楼	lóu	名	building
13	房间	fángjiān	名	room
14	电话	diànhuà	名	telephone
15	见	jiàn	动	to meet, to see

语法 | Grammar

1 序数词的用法
The use of ordinal numbers

序数词是表示次序的数词，表达方式一般为"第+数字"，可以和量词一起构成数量短语，修饰名词。数词后面也可以直接带名词，表示序数。

Ordinal numbers are numerals indicating orders, usually in the form of "第+number". They can form quantitative phrases with measure words to modify nouns. Numerals can also be put directly before nouns to act as ordinal numbers.

① Nǐ kàn, qiánbian dì-sān gè rén shì wǒ.
你看，前边第三个人是我。
Look, the third person in the front is me.

② Wǒ zhù zài xuéshēng sùshè wǔ hào lóu sān céng sān líng èr hào fángjiān.
我住在学生宿舍5号楼三层 302 号房间。
I live in room 302, on the third floor of Student Dormitory No. 5.

交际要点 | Communication Points

1 询问或说明某人的住址
Asking or telling someone's address

① Nǐ zhù zài nǎr?
你住在哪儿？
Where do you live?

② Wǒ zhù zài xuéshēng sùshè sān hào lóu.
我住在学生宿舍3号楼。
sān líng èr hào fángjiān.
302 号房间。
I live in room 302, Building 3 of Student Dormitory.

在描述详细的住址时，中国人习惯按照从大到小的顺序来说，即"城市—地区—路—小区—楼—房间号"。

When stating a detailed address, Chinese people follow a large-to-small sequence, i.e. "city-district-road-community-building-room number."

2 告别
Bidding farewell

Míngtiān jiàn.
明天见。
See you tomorrow.

"明天见"表示告别，在告别的同时可以简单说明下次见面的时间，可以根据实际情况替换"见"前边表示时间的词语，如"一会儿见""下午见"。

"明天见" (see you tomorrow) is used as to say good-bye and to specify the time when they will meet again. We can also replace "明天" (tomorrow) with other words, depending on the time of the next meeting, for example "一会儿见"(see you soon) and "下午见"(see you this afternoon).

第 2 课 LESSON TWO

课文 | Text

金太成与王杨通电话，让她参加宴会。 7-3

Kim Taesung is talking to Wang Yang on the phone, inviting her to attend a banquet.

Jīn Tàichéng 金 太 成	Yāo sān liù bā èr sì qī wǔ líng jiǔ jiǔ,　wèi,　Wáng Yáng ma? 13682475099，　　　　喂，王 杨 吗？ Wǒ shì Jīn Tàichéng. Nǐ xiànzài zài nǎr? 我是金太成。你现在在哪儿？
Wáng Yáng 王 杨	Nǐ hǎo, Jīn jīnglǐ. Wǒ zài jiāli. 你好，金经理。我在家里。
Jīn Tàichéng 金 太 成	Jīntiān wǎnshang yǒu yí gè yànhuì,　nǐ yě cānjiā ba. 今天 晚上 有一个宴会，你也参加吧。
Wáng Yáng 王 杨	Zài shénme dìfang? 在什么地方？
Jīn Tàichéng 金 太 成	Cháng'ān Fàndiàn. Wǒ xiànzài qù jiē nǐ. Nǐ zhù zài nǎr? 长安饭店。我现在去接你。你住在哪儿？
Wáng Yáng 王 杨	Wǒ zhù zài Yángguāng Xiǎoqū. 我住在阳光小区。
Jīn Tàichéng 金 太 成	Jǐ hào lóu? 几号楼？
Wáng Yáng 王 杨	Èrshísì hào lóu shíqī céng yāo qī líng bā hào. 24 号楼17 层 1708 号。
Jīn Tàichéng 金 太 成	Hǎo,　wǒ zài èrshísì hào lóu qiánbian děng nǐ. Yíhuìr jiàn. 好，我在 24 号楼前边等你。一会儿见。

生词 | New Words 7-4

1	喂	wèi	叹	hello
2	家	jiā	名	home, family
3	里	li	名	in (used after nouns and some monosyllabic adjectives to indicate place, time, limit, direction, etc)
4	今天	jīntiān	名	today
5	晚上	wǎnshang	名	evening
6	宴会	yànhuì	名	banquet
7	饭店	fàndiàn	名	hotel, restaurant
8	接	jiē	动	to pick up
9	小区	xiǎoqū	名	residential neighborhood
10	层	céng	量	floor of a building
11	前边	qiánbian	名	front
12	等	děng	动	to wait, to expect
13	一会儿	yíhuìr		a little while

专有名词 | Proper Nouns

14	长安饭店	Cháng'ān Fàndiàn		Chang'an Hotel
15	阳光小区	Yángguāng Xiǎoqū		Yangguang Residential Neighborhood

语法 | Grammar

2 方位的表达
The expression of direction and position

"在"和地点名词组合，再加上方位词如"上""下""前""后"和"边""面""头"等，用于表达方位。

"在", together with a noun of place, is used to express direction and position. Plus you can also use words such as "上", "下", "前", "后" and "边", "面", "头" to describe the proximity of a location.

Wǒ zài jiāli.
1 我**在家里**。
I'm at home.

Wǒ xiànzài zài xuéxiào.
2 我现在**在学校**。
I'm in school now.

Wǒ zài èrshísì lóu qiánbian děng nǐ.
3 我**在** 24 **楼前边**等你。
I'm waiting for you in front of Building 24.

Yínháng zài xuéxiào de zuǒbian.
4 银行**在学校的左边**。
The bank is located at the left side of the school.

第 3 课 LESSON THREE

课文 | Text

路口。玛丽向一位警察打听医院的地址。 7-5

At the intersection. Mary is asking a policeman about the location of a hospital.

玛丽　Qǐngwèn, Dì-èr Yīyuàn zài shénme dìfang?
　　　请问，第二医院在什么地方？

警察　Dì-èr Yīyuàn?
　　　第二医院？

玛丽　Duì.
　　　对。

警察　Zài Dōngchéng Lù shíwǔ hào.
　　　在东城路15号。

玛丽　Lí zhèr yuǎn bù yuǎn?
　　　离这儿远不远？

警察　Bú tài yuǎn. Nǐ zhīdào Cháng'ān Fàndiàn ma?
　　　不太远。你知道长安饭店吗？

玛丽　Wǒ zhīdào.
　　　我知道。

警察　Dì-èr Yīyuàn zài Cháng'ān Fàndiàn dōngbian.
　　　第二医院在长安饭店东边。

玛丽　Xièxie nǐ.
　　　谢谢你。

警察　Bié kèqi.
　　　别客气。

生词 | New Words 🔊 7-6

1	第二	dì-èr		the second
	第	dì	名	(used before numerals to form ordinal numbers)
	二	èr	数	two
2	医院	yīyuàn	名	hospital
3	路	lù	名	road
4	离	lí	动	to be away from
5	这儿	zhèr	代	here
6	远	yuǎn	形	far
7	知道	zhīdào	动	to know
8	东边	dōngbian	名	the east
9	别客气	bié kèqi		you are welcome
	别	bié	副	don't
	客气	kèqi	动	to be polite

专有名词 | Proper Nouns

10	第二医院	Dì-èr Yīyuàn	No. 2 Hospital
11	东城路	Dōngchéng Lù	Dongcheng Road

语法 | Grammar

3 "A+离+B+远/近"结构
The structure of "A+离+B+远/近"

"离"表示两个地方之间的距离,在这个结构中,"A 离 B"做主语。

"离" denotes the distance from one place to another. In this structure, "A 离 B" acts as the subject.

1. Běifāng Bīnguǎn lí zhèr bú tài yuǎn.
北方宾馆离这儿不太远。
Beifang Hotel is not too far from here.

2. Wǒ jiā lí xuéxiào hěn jìn.
我家离学校很近。
My home is very close to school.

3. Fàndiàn lí chēzhàn hěn yuǎn.
饭店离车站很远。
The hotel is very far from the station.

文化园 | Culture Corner

黄

河

The Yellow River

The Yellow River (黄河, Huánghé), the second longest river in China, is more than 5,460 kilometers in length. The Yellow River originates high up in the Qinghai-Tibet Plateau of Western China and flows down through 9 provinces and autonomous regions before emptying into the Bohai Sea in Shandong Province. Why is it named as the "yellow" river? It is because as it flows down from the Loess Plateau, the river becomes filled with silt from the ground, causing the color of the water to become yellow. There are two scenic places along the Yellow River that are absolute must-sees. The first one is the Hukou (Pot Mouth) Waterfalls, where a 300-meter-wide stretch of Yellow River suddenly narrows into a 30-meter-wide canyon and falls down 50 meters. The water rises and churns with great energy as it falls, as if pouring from the mouth of a teapot of incomparable size. It is for this reason that this natural wonder is called the Hukou (Pot Mouth) Waterfalls. The second site is the Xianglu (Incense Burner) Temple. This temple stands alone, with only one of its sides linked to an ancient city. Inside the ancient temple is a giant incense burner that is over 20 meters high and 5 meters in diameter, from which the temple derives its name. Viewing pictures of these two famous Yellow River sites will give you an experience of their magnificence, but truly comprehending their majesty requires actually visiting them and seeing them with your own eyes!

黄河是中国第二大河，全长约5,460公里，发源于中国西部的青藏高原，流经9个省自治区，最后从中国东部的山东省流入渤海。黄河为什么叫"黄"河呢？这是因为黄河上游流经黄土高原，大量的泥沙被带入河中，使河水的颜色变黄。黄河上有两大著名景观不能不看，一个是"壶口瀑布"，宽约300米的河水滚滚而来，流经大峡谷时突然被挤到仅有约30米宽，形成了约50米的落差，河水翻腾倾注，如同从巨大无比的壶中倒出，因此叫"壶口瀑布"。另一个是"香炉寺"，三面绝空，仅有一面与一座古城相通，一块直径约5米、高20多米的巨石好像一个硕大无比的香炉，因此得名。大家可以通过照片感受到这两处风景的壮观，但要真正领略其恢宏的气势，那就只有到现场了！

生词复习 | **Vocabulary Review**

1	比赛	bǐsài	competition
2	别客气	bié kèqi	you are welcome
	别	bié	don't
	客气	kèqi	to be polite
3	参加	cānjiā	to participate in
4	层	céng	floor of a building
5	当	dāng	to act as, to serve as
6	等	děng	to wait, to expect
7	第二	dì-èr	the second
	第	dì	(used before numerals to form ordinal numbers)
	二	èr	two
8	电话	diànhuà	telephone
9	东边	dōngbian	the east
10	饭店	fàndiàn	hotel, restaurant
11	房间	fángjiān	room
12	号	hào	number, order
13	家	jiā	home, family
14	见	jiàn	to meet, to see
15	健美操	jiànměicāo	callisthenics
16	接	jiē	to pick up
17	今天	jīntiān	today
18	离	lí	to be away from

19	里	li	in (used after nouns and some monosyllabic adjectives to indicate place, time, limit, direction, etc)
20	楼	lóu	building
21	路	lù	road
22	前边	qiánbian	front
23	去	qù	to go to
24	宿舍	sùshè	dormitory
25	晚上	wǎnshang	evening
26	喂	wèi	hello
27	我们	wǒmen	we, us
28	小区	xiǎoqū	residential neighborhood
29	学校	xuéxiào	school; university
30	宴会	yànhuì	banquet
31	医院	yīyuàn	hospital
32	一会儿	yíhuìr	a little while
33	有	yǒu	there be; to have
34	远	yuǎn	far
35	这儿	zhèr	here
36	知道	zhīdào	to know
37	住	zhù	to live
38	长安饭店	Cháng'ān Fàndiàn	Chang'an Hotel
39	第二医院	Dì-èr Yīyuàn	No. 2 Hospital
40	东城路	Dōngchéng Lù	Dongcheng Road
41	阳光小区	Yángguāng Xiǎoqū	Yangguang Residential Neighborhood

UNIT 8

Wǒ xǐhuan dà jiātíng.
我喜欢大家庭。
I like an extended family.

Objectives

In this unit, you'll learn:
- to inquire about family members
- to briefly introduce your family members

学习要点 | Key Points

Subject	Family
goals	Learn to inquire about and briefly introduce family members
Grammar points	• "了" at the end of a sentence • The expression of "only": 只有 • "有" sentences indicating possession • Using "和……一起"(together with…) and "一个人"(alone) as adverbial modifiers
Focal sentences	Inquiring about and introducing family members — A：你家（有）几口人？ B：我家（有）四口人。
	Expressing someone's wishes — 我爸爸希望我去银行工作。
	Making a simple description — 这个小区真漂亮。 真是个大家庭。
Words and phrases	家庭 口 四 妹妹 和 律师 非常 忙 常常 希望 银行 可是 医生 兄弟姐妹（兄弟、姐妹） 只 孩子 呢 姐姐 双胞胎 前面 就 送 父母 一起 都 爷爷 奶奶 哥哥 嫂子 他们 一共
Chinese characters	庭 口 四 妹 和 律 常 忙 希 望 银 行 医 生 兄 弟 只 孩 呢 双 胞 胎 面 送 父 母 起 都 爷 奶 哥 嫂 共

第 1 课 LESSON ONE

课文 | Text

公寓大厅。玛丽看外婆的照片。 🔊 8-1

At the lobby of an apartment building. Mary is looking at her grandmother's picture.

Fēi yǎ		Xiǎng wàipó le?
菲雅		想外婆了？
Mǎ lì		Duì, wǒ māma shuō wàipó zài Běijīng.
玛丽		对，我妈妈说外婆在北京。
Fēi yǎ		Nǐ jiā yǒu jǐ kǒu rén?
菲雅		你家有几口人？
Mǎ lì		Wǒ jiā yǒu sì kǒu rén, bàba, māma, mèimei hé wǒ.
玛丽		我家有四口人，爸爸、妈妈、妹妹和我。
Fēi yǎ		À, nǐ hái yǒu gè mèimei! Tā duō dà le?
菲雅		啊，你还有个妹妹！她多大了？
Mǎ lì		Tā jīnnián shíbā suì, shì gè dàxuéshēng.
玛丽		她今年18岁，是个大学生。
Fēi yǎ		Nǐ bàba zuò shénme gōngzuò?
菲雅		你爸爸做什么工作？
Mǎ lì		Tā shì lǜshī. Tā fēicháng máng, chángcháng bú zài jiā.
玛丽		他是律师。他非常忙，常常不在家。
Fēi yǎ		Nǐ māma yě gōngzuò ma?
菲雅		你妈妈也工作吗？
Mǎ lì		Yě gōngzuò, tā shì lǎoshī.
玛丽		也工作，她是老师。

生词 | New Words 〔8-2〕

1	口	kǒu	量	(measure word, used for family members)
2	四	sì	数	four
3	妹妹	mèimei	名	younger sister
4	和	hé	连	and
5	律师	lùshī	名	lawyer
6	非常	fēicháng	副	very, extremely
7	忙	máng	形	busy
8	常常	chángcháng	副	often

语法 | Grammar

1 句尾"了"
"了" at the end of a sentence

语气助词"了"用在句尾，表示事态出现了变化或即将出现变化，有成句的作用。

The modal particle "了" is placed at the end of a sentence, mainly to denote changes in the situation and complete the sentence.

① Lǐ Míng liù suì le.
李明 6 岁了。
Li Ming is 6 years old.

② Tā mèimei jīnnián shíbā suì le, shì gè dàxuéshēng.
她妹妹今年 18 岁了，是个大学生。
Her younger sister is 18-year-old, and is a university student.

交际要点 | Communication Points

询问或说明家庭成员
Inquiring about and introducing family members

① Nǐ jiā yǒu jǐ kǒu rén?
你家(有)几口人？
How many people are there in your family?

② Wǒ jiā yǒu sì kǒu rén, bàba, māma, mèimei hé wǒ.
我家有四口人，爸爸、妈妈、妹妹和我。
There are four people in my family, my father, my mother, my younger sister and me.

量词"口"多用在"人"前面。"几口人"用于询问家庭成员的数量，回答时，通常会将家庭成员按照年龄大小进行排列。

The measure word "口" is commonly used before "人". "几口人"(how many people) is used to ask how many people in someone's family. The respondent usually lists family members in order of age.

第 2 课 LESSON TWO

课文 | Text

咖啡厅。张圆圆和麦克在聊天儿。 8-3

At the coffeehouse. Zhang Yuanyuan and Mike are chatting.

Zhāng Yuányuan / 张圆圆: Màikè, nǐ zài Měiguó gōngzuò ma?
麦克，你在美国工作吗？

Màikè / 麦克: Wǒ bù gōngzuò. Wǒ bàba xīwàng wǒ qù yínháng gōngzuò, kěshì wǒ bù xǐhuan.
我不工作。我爸爸希望我去银行工作，可是我不喜欢。

Zhāng Yuányuan / 张圆圆: Nǐ bàba zuò shénme gōngzuò?
你爸爸做什么工作？

Màikè / 麦克: Wǒ bàba shì gè yīshēng.
我爸爸是个医生。

Zhāng Yuányuan / 张圆圆: Nǐ yǒu xiōngdì jiěmèi ma?
你有兄弟姐妹吗？

Màikè / 麦克: Wǒ jiā zhǐ yǒu wǒ yí gè háizi. Nǐ ne?
我家只有我一个孩子。你呢？

Zhāng Yuányuan / 张圆圆: Wǒ yǒu yí gè jiějie.
我有一个姐姐。

Màikè / 麦克: Tā jīnnián duō dà?
她今年多大？

Zhāng Yuányuan / 张圆圆: Tā yě èrshíyī suì, wǒmen shì shuāngbāotāi.
她也21岁，我们是双胞胎。

Màikè / 麦克: Tā yě hěn piàoliang ba?
她也很漂亮吧？

生词 | New Words 8-4

1	希望	xīwàng	动	to hope, to wish
2	银行	yínháng	名	bank
3	可是	kěshì	连	but
4	医生	yīshēng	名	doctor
5	兄弟姐妹	xiōngdì jiěmèi		brothers and sisters
	兄弟	xiōngdì	名	brothers
	姐妹	jiěmèi	名	sisters
6	只	zhǐ	副	only
7	孩子	háizi	名	child
8	呢	ne	助	(auxiliary word)
9	姐姐	jiějie	名	elder sister
10	双胞胎	shuāngbāotāi	名	twins

语法 | Grammar

2 "唯一"的表达：只有
The expression of "only": 只有

"只有"表示除此以外没有别的，限制与动作有关的事物的数量。

"只有" denotes that there is no other exception other than the one mentioned, restricting the quantity of objects related to the action.

1 Màikè jiā zhǐyǒu tā yí gè háizi.
麦克家**只有**他一个孩子。
Mike is the only child in his family.

2 Xiànzài wǒ zhǐyǒu yí gè Zhōngguó péngyou.
现在我**只有**一个中国朋友。
Right now I only have one Chinese friend.

3 表示领属关系的"有"字句
"有" sentences indicating possession

由"有"做谓语动词，用于表示领有或存在的句子，叫"有"字句。其句型一般为"名词1+有+名词2"，其否定形式是在"有"的前面加"没"。

A "有" sentence refers to a sentence with "有" as its predicate, and it is used to show possession or existence. Its structure is "noun 1+有+noun 2". The negative form is to add a "没" before "有".

1 Wǒ jiā yǒu wǔ kǒu rén.
我家**有**五口人。
There are five people in my family.

2 Zhāng Yuányuan yǒu yí gè jiějie.
张圆圆**有**一个姐姐。
Zhang Yuanyuan has one elder sister.

3 Màikè méi yǒu xiōngdì jiěmèi.
麦克**没有**兄弟姐妹。
Mike doesn't have any brothers or sisters.

第 3 课 LESSON THREE

课文 | Text

宴会结束后,金太成送王杨回阳光小区。

After the banquet. Kim Taesung drives Wang Yang back to Yangguang Residential Neighborhood.

王杨 (Wáng Yáng): Qiánmiàn jiù shì Yángguāng Xiǎoqū. Xièxie nǐ sòng wǒ.
前面就是阳光小区。谢谢你送我。

金太成 (Jīn Tàichéng): Zhège xiǎoqū zhēn piàoliang. Nǐ yí gè rén zhù ma?
这个小区真漂亮。你一个人住吗?

王杨 (Wáng Yáng): Bù, wǒ hé fùmǔ yìqǐ zhù. Nǐ ne?
不,我和父母一起住。你呢?

金太成 (Jīn Tàichéng): Xiànzài wǒ yí gè rén zhù. Wǒ jiārén dōu zài Hánguó.
现在我一个人住。我家人都在韩国。

王杨 (Wáng Yáng): Nǐ jiā dōu yǒu shénme rén?
你家都有什么人?

金太成 (Jīn Tàichéng): Yéye, nǎinai, bàba, māma, hái yǒu gēge, sǎozi hé tāmen de háizi, yígòng shí kǒu rén.
爷爷、奶奶、爸爸、妈妈,还有哥哥、嫂子和他们的孩子,一共十口人。

王杨 (Wáng Yáng): Zhēn shì gè dà jiātíng. Nǐmen dōu zhù zài yìqǐ ma?
真是个大家庭。你们都住在一起吗?

金太成 (Jīn Tàichéng): Duì, dōu zhù zài yìqǐ.
对,都住在一起。

生词 | New Words 🔊 8-6

1	前面	qiánmiàn	名	front
2	就	jiù	副	just
3	送	sòng	动	to escort
4	父母	fùmǔ	名	parents
5	一起	yìqǐ	副	together
6	都	dōu	副	all
7	爷爷	yéye	名	grandpa
8	奶奶	nǎinai	名	grandma
9	哥哥	gēge	名	elder brother
10	嫂子	sǎozi	名	sister-in-law (wife of your elder brother)
11	他们	tāmen	代	they
12	一共	yígòng	副	altogether
13	家庭	jiātíng	名	family

语法 | Grammar

4 "和……一起" "一个人" 作状语
Using "和……一起" (together with...) and "一个人" (alone) as adverbial modifiers

"和……一起"作状语，表示在同一地点或合到一处，强调空间上的共同。"一个人"作状语，表示单独、自己。

"和……一起" as an adverbial modifier means to be together with someone in the same place, emphasizing being together in space. "一个人" as an adverbial modifier indicates being "alone" or "by oneself".

① Wáng Yáng hé fùmǔ yìqǐ zhù.
王杨和父母一起住。
Wang Yang lives with her parents.

② Wǒ míngtiān hé nǐ yìqǐ qù xuéxiào.
我明天和你一起去学校。
I'll go to school with you tomorrow.

③ Zài Běijīng, Jīn Tàichéng yí gè rén zhù.
在北京，金太成一个人住。
Kim Taesung lives alone in Beijing.

④ Jīntiān tā yí gè rén zài jiā.
今天她一个人在家。
Today she was alone at home.

文化园 | Culture Corner

家庭生活

Family Life

Family is an important unit of society. Around 50 years ago, Chinese families were centered around large clans, with a large number of relations living together. This was typically involved three generations: grandparents, parents and young children all lived within the same household. Some families even had the fortune of having four generations under the same roof. As society has developed, the clan-based system has given way to the smaller family unit that consists only of parents and their non-adult children. Nowadays after the children get married, they would not continue to reside with their parents, instead they move out to setup their own family in a separate dwelling. However, the notion of a clan-based family has not entirely vanished. During each important festival, family members will get together from all directions. Besides, since in over 60% of households both husband and wife work, many elderly people would care for the third generations after they get retired. Outside the elementary school, you will see a lot of elderly people in their 60s waiting to pick up their grandsons and granddaughters after school.

家庭是社会的重要组成部分。大约50年以前，中国的家庭是以大家族的形式存在的，即同一个家族的人生活在一起，一般以三代为多，爷爷奶奶、爸爸妈妈和孩子们。偶尔也有"四世同堂"的情况。随着社会的发展，现在的中国家庭一般是父母和未成年子女一起生活，子女一旦结婚，就会搬出去独立生活，形成一个新的家庭模式。但是，大家族的观念并没有因此而消失。每到重要节日，人们都会从四面八方团聚到一起。另外，由于在60%以上的中国家庭中，夫妻双方都工作，很多老人退休以后会帮助子女照顾第三代。小学放学的时候，你会看到很多60岁左右的老人，在学校门口等着接孙子、孙女。

生词复习 | Vocabulary Review

1	常常	chángcháng	often
2	都	dōu	all
3	非常	fēicháng	very, extremely
4	父母	fùmǔ	parents
5	哥哥	gēge	elder brother
6	孩子	háizi	child
7	和	hé	and
8	家庭	jiātíng	family
9	姐姐	jiějie	elder sister
10	就	jiù	just
11	可是	kěshì	but
12	口	kǒu	(measure word, used for family members)
13	律师	lǜshī	lawyer
14	忙	máng	busy
15	妹妹	mèimei	younger sister
16	奶奶	nǎinai	grandma
17	呢	ne	(auxiliary word)
18	前面	qiánmiàn	front
19	嫂子	sǎozi	sister-in-law (wife of your elder brother)
20	双胞胎	shuāngbāotāi	twins
21	四	sì	four
22	送	sòng	to escort
23	他们	tāmen	they
24	希望	xīwàng	to hope, to wish
25	兄弟姐妹	xiōngdì jiěmèi	brothers and sisters
	兄弟	xiōngdì	brothers
	姐妹	jiěmèi	sisters
26	爷爷	yéye	grandpa
27	医生	yīshēng	doctor
28	一共	yígòng	altogether
29	一起	yìqǐ	together
30	银行	yínháng	bank
31	只	zhǐ	only

UNIT 9

Wǒ zuìjìn hěn máng.
我最近很忙。
I've been very busy recently.

Objectives

In this unit, you'll learn:
- to ask and tell the time with simple words
- to describe someone's daily routine

学习要点 | Key Points

Subject	Time
Goals	Learn to ask and tell the time, and describe someone's daily routine with simple words
Grammar Points	• Point in time+"了" • Questions with "几点"(what time) and "什么时候"(when) • Adverbials of time: point in time+verb phrase; point in time+以前(before)/以后(after)+verb phrase
Focal Sentences	Asking and telling about the time — A：现在几点？ B：现在 10 点 20。
	Courtesy to make inquiries — 请问，现在几点？ 对不起，几点了？ 劳驾，第二医院在哪儿？
	Telling someone what to do at a certain time — 我每天 6 点起床。
	Expressing uncertainty — 不一定。
Words and Phrases	最近 点 半 劳驾 分 姑娘 差 愿意 能 时候 下班 行 到 吃 晚饭 开始 训练 先生 起床 以后 睡觉 这么 上班 加班 总公司 项 重要 不一定 有时候 星期五 有空儿 再说
Chinese Characters	最 近 点 半 劳 驾 分 姑 娘 差 愿 意 能 候 班 行 到 吃 饭 开 始 训 练 先 床 以 后 睡 觉 加 总 项 重 定 五 空 再

第1课 LESSON ONE

课文 | Text

玛丽在公园画画，游客走过来问时间。 9-1
Mary is drawing a picture in a park when some tourists come over and ask her about the time.

	Yóukè yī	Qǐngwèn, xiànzài jǐ diǎn?
游客1		请问，现在几点？
	Mǎ lì	Xiànzài shí diǎn èrshí.
玛丽		现在10点20。
	Yóukè èr	Duìbuqǐ, xiànzài jǐ diǎn?
游客2		对不起，现在几点？
	Mǎ lì	Shí diǎn bàn.
玛丽		10点半。
	Yóukè sān	Láojià, jǐ diǎn le?
游客3		劳驾，几点了？
	Mǎ lì	Shí diǎn wǔshí le.
玛丽		10点50了。
	Yóukè sì	Duìbuqǐ, xiànzài jǐ diǎn?
游客4		对不起，现在几点？
	Mǎ lì	Shíyī diǎn wǔ fēn le.
玛丽		11点5分了。

玛丽贴了一张纸条：我不知道现在几点！
Mary puts up a piece of paper: I don't know the time!

45 分钟后。
45 minutes later.

	Yóukè wǔ	Gūniang, xiànzài chà shí fēn shí'èr diǎn.
游客5		姑娘，现在差10分12点。
	Mǎ lì	
玛丽		……

生词 | New Words 🎧 9-2

1	点	diǎn	量	o'clock, hour (measure word)
2	半	bàn	数	half
3	劳驾	láojià	动	excuse me
4	分	fēn	量	minute (measure word)
5	姑娘	gūniang	名	young lady
6	差	chà	动	to be less than, to be short of

语法 | Grammar

1 时间点+了
Point in time+"了"

语气助词"了"用在句尾，表示事态出现了变化或即将出现变化，有成句的作用。"时间点+了"表示这个时间点到了。

The modal particle "了" is placed at the end of a sentence, mainly to denote changes in the situation and complete the sentence. "Point in time+了" indicates the arrival of the point in time.

Shí diǎn wǔshí fēn le.
10 点 50 分 了。
It's 10:50.

交际要点 | Communication Points

1 询问时的礼貌用语
Courtesy to make inquires

Qǐngwèn, xiànzài jǐ diǎn?
① 请问，现在几点？
Excuse me, what's the time now?

Duìbuqǐ, xiànzài jǐ diǎn?
② 对不起，现在几点？
Excuse me, what's the time now?

"请问""劳驾""对不起""不好意思"可以作为询问时的礼貌用语放在句首，后边接问句，例如"请问，现在几点？"

When making an inquiry, "请问", "劳驾", "对不起" and "不好意思" can all be put at the beginning of an interrogative sentence as a courtesy. For example, "请问，现在几点？"(Excuse me, what's the time now?)

第 2 课 LESSON TWO

课文 | Text

学校排练场。麦克和张圆圆在约定训练时间。 9-3

At the drill ground of the university. Mike and Zhang Yuanyuan are discussing the time for their training.

Zhāng Yuányuan		Nǐ kàn zěnmeyàng?
张 圆 圆		你看怎么样？
Mài kè		Búcuò. Wǒ yuànyì dāng nǐmen de jiàoliàn.
麦 克		不错。我愿意当你们的教练。
Zhāng Yuányuan		Míngtiān nǐ néng lái ma?
张 圆 圆		明天你能来吗？
Mài kè		Shénme shíhou?
麦 克		什么时候？
Zhāng Yuányuan		Xiàwǔ sān diǎn, hǎo ma?
张 圆 圆		下午3点，好吗？
Mài kè		Wǒ xiàwǔ sān diǎn gōngzuò, wǔ diǎn bàn xiàbān. Liù diǎn kěyǐ ma?
麦 克		我下午3点工作，5点半下班。6点可以吗？
Zhāng Yuányuan		Liù diǎn bù xíng. Wǒmen wǔ diǎn bàn dào liù diǎn bàn chī wǎnfàn.
张 圆 圆		6点不行。我们5点半到6点半吃晚饭。
Mài kè		Nà wǒ qī diǎn dào ba. Qī diǎn bàn kāishǐ xùnliàn.
麦 克		那我7点到吧。7点半开始训练。
Zhāng Yuányuan		Tài hǎo le, xièxie nǐ!
张 圆 圆		太好了，谢谢你！

生词 | New Words 9-4

1	愿意	yuànyì	动	to be willing to
2	能	néng	动	to be able to
3	时候	shíhou	名	time, moment
4	下班	xiàbān	动	to be off duty, to get off work
5	行	xíng	动	will do
6	到	dào	动	to arrive, to reach
7	吃	chī	动	to eat
8	晚饭	wǎnfàn	名	supper
9	开始	kāishǐ	动	to start
10	训练	xùnliàn	动	to train

语法 | Grammar

2 用"几点"和"什么时候"的疑问句
Questions with "几点"(what time) and "什么时候"(when)

特指问句指用疑问代词提问的疑问句。"几点""什么时候"等可以充当句子的谓语、状语等，用以询问时间。

Specific interrogation refers to a sentence where an interrogative pronoun is used to raise a question. "几点" and "什么时候" can act as a predicate or adverbial modifier to ask about time.

1. Qǐngwèn, xiànzài jǐ diǎn?
   请问，现在几点？
   Excuse me, what time is it?

2. Nǐ shénme shíhou yǒu kòngr?
   你什么时候有空儿？
   When are you available?

交际要点 | Communication Points

2 征求或询问某人的意见
Asking for someone's opinions

Nǐ kàn zěnmeyàng?
你看怎么样？
What do you think?

用于表示征求或询问某人的意见，可以在动词"看"和"怎么样"之间加上具体的事物，即"你看……怎么样？"这里的"看"是观察并加以判断的意思。还可以说"你觉得……怎么样？"

It is used to seek or ask for others' opinions and specific items can be added between "看" (here means "to think") and "怎么样", i.e. "你看……怎么样？"(What do you think of...?). "你觉得……怎么样？" (How do you feel about...?) can also be used to express the same meaning.

第 3 课 LESSON THREE

课文 | Text

校园餐厅。山口和子和金太成在谈作息时间。

At the cafeteria on campus. Yamaguchi Kazuko and Kim Taesung are talking about their daily routines.

山口和子 (Shānkǒu Hézǐ): 金先生，你最近很忙吧？
Jīn xiānsheng, nǐ zuìjìn hěn máng ba?

金太成 (Jīn Tàichéng): 对，我最近非常忙。每天6点起床，晚上12点以后睡觉。
Duì, wǒ zuìjìn fēicháng máng. Měi tiān liù diǎn qǐchuáng, wǎnshang shí'èr diǎn yǐhòu shuìjiào.

山口和子 (Shānkǒu Hézǐ): 这么忙？
Zhème máng?

金太成 (Jīn Tàichéng): 上午学习汉语，下午去公司上班，最近晚上还要加班。
Shàngwǔ xuéxí Hànyǔ, xiàwǔ qù gōngsī shàngbān, zuìjìn wǎnshang hái yào jiābān.

山口和子 (Shānkǒu Hézǐ): 加班？
Jiābān?

金太成 (Jīn Tàichéng): 对，总公司给了我一项重要的工作。
Duì, zǒnggōngsī gěi le wǒ yí xiàng zhòngyào de gōngzuò.

山口和子 (Shānkǒu Hézǐ): 你每天几点下班？
Nǐ měi tiān jǐ diǎn xiàbān?

金太成 (Jīn Tàichéng): 不一定，有时候8点，有时候10点。
Bùyídìng, yǒushíhou bā diǎn, yǒushíhou shí diǎn.

山口和子 (Shānkǒu Hézǐ): 我想和你一起吃晚饭。你星期五晚上有空儿吗？
Wǒ xiǎng hé nǐ yìqǐ chī wǎnfàn. Nǐ Xīngqīwǔ wǎnshang yǒu kòngr ma?

金太成 (Jīn Tàichéng): 再说吧。
Zàishuō ba.

生词 | New Words

#				
1	先生	xiānsheng	名	Mr
2	最近	zuìjìn	名	lately, recently
3	起床	qǐchuáng	动	to get up
4	以后	yǐhòu	名	later, after
5	睡觉	shuìjiào	动	to sleep
6	这么	zhème	代	such, so
7	上班	shàngbān	动	to go to work
8	加班	jiābān	动	to work overtime
9	总公司	zǒnggōngsī	名	head office
10	项	xiàng	量	(measure word)
11	重要	zhòngyào	形	important
12	不一定	bùyídìng	副	not sure
13	有时候	yǒushíhou	副	sometimes, occasionally
14	星期五	Xīngqīwǔ	名	Friday
15	有空儿	yǒu kòngr		to be free
16	再说	zàishuō	动	to put off until some time later

语法 | Grammar

3 时间状语：时间点＋动词短语；时间点＋以前/以后＋动词短语
Adverbials of time: point in time+verb phrase; point in time+ 以前 (before)/ 以后 (after)+verb phrase

需要注意两点：时间点前面没有"在"，动词短语要放在时间点之后而不是之前。

Attention should be paid to two aspects: There is not "在" before the point in time; verb phrases should be placed after a point in time.

Wǒ měi tiān liù diǎn qǐchuáng, wǎnshang shí'èr diǎn yǐhòu shuìjiào.
我每天6点起床，晚上12点以后睡觉。
I get up at 6:00 every morning and go to sleep after 12:00 every night.

交际要点 | Communication Points

3 委婉地推辞
Polite refusal

Zàishuō ba.
再说吧。
Let's discuss it later.

中国人不喜欢直接拒绝别人，一般都会采用间接的方式，委婉地拒绝他人。"再说吧"就是很典型的句子，表示现在不行，以后再讨论。

Chinese people prefer not to refuse or turn others down in a direct way. "再说吧" (we'll discuss it later) expresses that the speaker does not want to discuss a certain topic at the moment and he/she wants to talk about it later.

文化园 | Culture Corner

烤鸭

北京有很多好吃的菜，比较受欢迎的是"烤鸭"，因此又叫"北京烤鸭"。既然叫"烤鸭"，那一定得"烤"吧？对啦！做烤鸭除了要有品质很好的鸭子，还要有一个大大的烤炉。鸭子在经过多道工序处理好以后，就被一个一个地挂到炉子里的四周，下面堆放果木作为燃料，果木燃烧产生的热量，把鸭子烤得满身流油，香气四溢。常用的果木有枣树、桃树、杏树等，它们带有一定的香味，用这样的果木烤制的鸭子不但色泽红润，而且肉质香酥，特别好吃！北京的烤鸭店很多，最有名的是"全聚德"，如果你有机会到北京来，可一定得去尝尝啊！

Roast Duck

Beijing has many delicious dishes, one of the most popular of which is its roast duck. Therefore, this dish is known as "Beijing Roast Duck". Given the name of this dish, is it actually "roasted"? Of course! In order to make roast duck, you not only need duck of the finest quality, but also must have an enormous roasting oven. After the ducks have been prepared through a range of preliminary procedures, they are hung all around the insides of the enormous oven over a pile of smoldering fruit tree wood, which serves as the fuel for roasting. The heat generated by this burning wood cooks the duck in a way that allows its natural oils to seep to the surface, suffusing an exquisite fragrance all around. Commonly used fruit woods include jujube tree wood, peach tree wood and apricot tree wood. These woods are very fragrant, leaving the duck meat with a rosy color and crisp-fried on the outside, all of which makes the duck absolutely delicious! There are many roast duck restaurants in Beijing, the most famous of which is "全聚德" (Quánjùdé). If you have the chance to go to Beijing, you are strongly recommended to go and try the duck for yourself!

生词复习 | Vocabulary Review

#	汉字	Pinyin	English
1	半	bàn	half
2	不一定	bùyídìng	not sure
3	差	chà	to be less than, to be short of
4	吃	chī	to eat
5	到	dào	to arrive, to reach
6	点	diǎn	o'clock, hour (measure word)
7	分	fēn	minute (measure word)
8	姑娘	gūniang	young lady
9	加班	jiābān	to work overtime
10	开始	kāishǐ	to start
11	劳驾	láojià	excuse me
12	能	néng	to be able to
13	起床	qǐchuáng	to get up
14	上班	shàngbān	to go to work
15	时候	shíhou	time, moment
16	睡觉	shuìjiào	to sleep
17	晚饭	wǎnfàn	supper
18	下班	xiàbān	to be off duty, to get off work
19	先生	xiānsheng	Mr
20	项	xiàng	(measure word)
21	星期五	Xīngqīwǔ	Friday
22	行	xíng	will do
23	训练	xùnliàn	to train
24	以后	yǐhòu	later, after
25	有空儿	yǒu kòngr	to be free
26	有时候	yǒushíhou	sometimes, occasionally
27	愿意	yuànyì	to be willing to
28	再说	zàishuō	to put off until some time later
29	这么	zhème	such, so
30	重要	zhòngyào	important
31	总公司	zǒnggōngsī	head office
32	最近	zuìjìn	lately, recently

UNIT 10

Wǒ lái jièshào yíxià.
我来介绍一下。
Let me introduce.

Objectives

In this unit, you'll learn:
- to briefly introduce someone's basic information
- to make an appointment with someone

学习要点 | Key Points

Subject	Basic personal information
Goals	Learn to briefly introduce someone's basic information and make an appointment with someone
Grammar Points	• Sentences with adjectival predicates
Focal sentences	Introducing A and B to each other — 我来介绍一下。这是麦克，我的健身教练。这是我姐姐张芳芳。 Telling about someone's daily routine — 我们星期三下午 3 点半去健身。 Telling one's address — 我住在 6 号楼 433 房间。 Asking if someone is free — 你什么时候有时间？
Words and Phrases	真的　没什么　欢迎　下次（下、次）　星期三 好的　朋友　女儿　学　教　时间　没有　课　给　打
Chinese Characters	真　迎　次　三　教　间　课　打

第 1 课 LESSON ONE

课文 | Text

咖啡厅。张圆圆向张芳芳介绍麦克。 ▶10-1
At the coffeehouse. Zhang Yuanyuan is introducing Mike to Zhang Fangfang.

Zhāng Yuányuan	Fāngfāng, wǒ lái jièshào yíxià, zhè shì Màikè, wǒ de jiànshēn jiàoliàn.	
张 圆 圆	芳芳，我来介绍一下，这是麦克，我的健身教练。	
	Màikè, zhè shì wǒ jiějie Zhāng Fāngfāng.	
	麦克，这是我姐姐张 芳芳。	
Mài kè	Nǐ hǎo, Fāngfāng! Rènshi nǐ hěn gāoxìng.	
麦 克	你好，芳芳！认识你很 高兴。	
Zhāng Fāngfāng	Nǐ hǎo, Màikè! (duì Zhāng Yuányuan) Zhēn de hěn shuài!	
张 芳 芳	你好，麦克！（对张 圆圆）真的很帅！	
Mài kè	Nǐ shuō shénme?	
麦 克	你说什么？	
Zhāng Yuányuan	Méi shénme, méi shénme. Fāngfāng yě xiǎng jiànshēn.	
张 圆 圆	没什么、没什么。芳芳也想 健身。	
Mài kè	Huānyíng, huānyíng. Nǐmen kěyǐ yìqǐ qù.	
麦 克	欢迎，欢迎。你们可以一起去。	
Zhāng Fāngfāng	Xià cì nǐ shénme shíhou qù jiànshēn?	
张 芳 芳	下次你什么时候去健身？	
Zhāng Yuányuan	Xīngqīsān xiàwǔ sān diǎn bàn.	
张 圆 圆	星期三下午3点半。	
Zhāng Fāngfāng	Hǎo de. Wǒmen yìqǐ qù.	
张 芳 芳	好的。我们一起去。

生词 | New Words 🔊 10-2

1	真的	zhēn de		really
2	没什么	méi shénme		nothing
3	欢迎	huānyíng	动	to welcome
4	下次	xià cì		next time
	下	xià	名	next
	次	cì	量	time (measure word)
5	星期三	Xīngqīsān	名	Wednesday
6	好的	hǎo de		OK

语法 | Grammar

形容词谓语句
Sentences with adjectival predicates

　　形容词可以做谓语。单个形容词做谓语带有比较或对照的意味，加上"很""非常""真"等词则表示事物性状或人的某个特点的程度。

　　Adjectives can be used as predicates. A single adjective as a predicate denotes comparison or contrast; when used together with "很"(very), "非常"(very), "真"(really), etc, it indicates the degree of the properties of a person or a thing.

Tā hěn shuài.
1 他 **很 帅**。
He's very handsome.

Nǐ de shēngyīn zhēn hǎotīng!
2 你 的 声 音 **真 好 听**！
You have a really nice voice!

交际要点 | Communication Points

时间的表达方法
Expressing the time

Xīngqīsān xiàwǔ sān diǎn bàn
星期三下午3点半。
3:30 p.m. on Wednesday.

中国人在表述时间时，通常按照"从大到小"的顺序，描述的内容越来越具体，即"星期+早上/上午/下午/晚上+钟点"。

Chinese people always follow the "large-to-small" and "general-to-specific" sequences to describe time, i.e. "week+early morning/morning/afternoon/evening+point in time".

第 2 课 LESSON TWO

课文 | Text

校园大门口。菲雅与李冬生、陈晓红相遇。 ▶10-3

At the campus gate. Faye comes across Li Dongsheng and Chen Xiaohong.

菲雅 Nǐ hǎo, Lǐ lǎoshī!
你好，李老师！

李冬生 Nǐ hǎo! Wǒ lái jièshào yíxià, zhè shì Fēiyǎ, wǒ de xuésheng.
你好！我来介绍一下，这是菲雅，我的学生。

Zhè shì Chén Xiǎohóng, Chén lǎoshī.
这是陈晓红，陈老师。

菲雅 Nǐ hǎo, Chén lǎoshī!
你好，陈老师！

陈晓红 Nǐ hǎo, Fēiyǎ! Nǐ shì nǎ guó rén?
你好，菲雅！你是哪国人？

菲雅 Wǒ shì Yìnní rén.
我是印尼人。

陈晓红 Nǐ zài xuéxiào zhù ma?
你在学校住吗？

菲雅 Duì, wǒ zhù zài liù hào lóu sì sān sān fángjiān.
对，我住在6号楼433房间。

Chén lǎoshī, nǐ yě shì Hànyǔ lǎoshī ma?
陈老师，你也是汉语老师吗？

陈晓红 Bù, wǒ shì Fǎyǔ lǎoshī.
不，我是法语老师。

菲雅 Nǐmen shì péngyou?
你们是朋友？

李冬生 Shì. Tā shì wǒ lǎoshī de nǚ'ér.
是。她是我老师的女儿。

菲雅 Ō.
噢。

Unit 10 Lesson Two

生词 | New Words 🔊 10-4

1	朋友	péngyou	名	friend
2	女儿	nǚ'ér	名	daughter

第 3 课 LESSON THREE

课文 | Text

在戏剧彩排室。艺术家赵玉兰和玛丽在交谈。
At the drama rehearsal room. The artist Zhao Yulan and Mary are chatting.

Mǎ lì	Zhào lǎoshī, nín jīnnián duō dà niánjì?	
玛 丽	赵老师，您今年多大年纪？	
Zhào Yùlán	Wǒ jīnnián sìshíbā suì. Nǐ ne?	
赵玉兰	我今年 48 岁。你呢？	
Mǎ lì	Èrshí'èr suì. Wǒ xiǎng xué jīngjù, nín jiāojiao wǒ, hǎo ma?	
玛 丽	22 岁。我想学京剧，您教教我，好吗？	
Zhào Yùlán	Kěyǐ a!	
赵玉兰	可以啊！	
Mǎ lì	Nín shénme shíhou yǒu shíjiān?	
玛 丽	您什么时候有时间？	
Zhào Yùlán	Wǒ měi tiān xiàwǔ dōu yǒu shíjiān.	
赵玉兰	我每天下午都有时间。	
Mǎ lì	Wǒ xiàwǔ méiyǒu kè. Wǒ gěi nín dǎ diànhuà ba.	
玛 丽	我下午没有课。我给您打电话吧。	
Zhào Yùlán	Hǎo de, wǒ de diànhuà shì liù yāo qī jiǔ sì èr qī qī.	
赵玉兰	好的，我的电话是 61794277。	
Mǎ lì	Liù qī yāo jiǔ sì qī èr qī.	
玛 丽	67194727。	
Zhào Yùlán	Shì liù yāo qī jiǔ sì èr qī qī.	
赵玉兰	是 61794277。	

生词 | New Words 10-6

1	学	xué	动	to learn
2	教	jiāo	动	to teach
3	时间	shí jiān	名	time
4	没有	méiyǒu	动	not to have, to be without
5	课	kè	名	lesson, class
6	给	gěi	介	to, for
7	打	dǎ	动	to make (a phone call)

文化园 | **Culture Corner**

汉
字

Chinese Characters

Many foreigners are keen to know how Chinese people manage to effortlessly identify thousands of Chinese characters which look like drawings. For foreigners, characters resemble pictures, so they mistakenly think that all characters are pictographic in nature. This is a misconception. Actually the real pictographic characters are rare in the Chinese writing system. This is because "shape" can only convey simple meanings and cannot be relied on to articulate the complexity of economics, nor the cultures of human society. For this reason, Chinese people found a solution in the Chinese script by developing a kind of "compounds", combining form, sound and meaning. Character "compounds" were borrowed and transferred to convey novel words in written form, thereby allowing the number of possible Chinese characters to multiply. Given their combination of form, sound and meaning, reading Chinese makes people be not only able to enjoy the pleasure of sound but also able to taste the subtle connotations of the characters. This provides the reader with an excellent opportunity to exercise his mind. Don't you want to give it a try?

很多外国人特别想知道，中国人是用什么办法非常轻松地从众多如画一般的汉字中找到自己需要的那一个的。外国人看汉字像图画，以为所有的汉字都是象形字，这是一种错觉。其实真正的象形字并不多，因为"形"只能表示简单的意思，无法表达经济、文化、思想类的复杂含义，但中国人找到了很好的办法，那就是"复合"汉字，把"形""声""意"结合起来，甚至还可以"借用"或者"转释"，这样，可以使用的字就多了起来。中国人使用汉字不仅可以享受到声音的乐趣，还能体会到"字义"的内涵，这对大脑来说，也是一个锻炼的好机会。你不想体验一下吗？

生词复习 | **Vocabulary Review**

1	打	dǎ	to make (a phone call)
2	给	gěi	to, for
3	好的	hǎo de	OK
4	欢迎	huānyíng	to welcome
5	教	jiāo	to teach
6	课	kè	lesson, class
7	没什么	méi shénme	nothing
8	没有	méiyǒu	not to have, to be without
9	女儿	nǚ'ér	daughter
10	朋友	péngyou	friend
11	时间	shíjiān	time
12	下次	xià cì	next time
	下	xià	next
	次	cì	time (measure word)
13	星期三	Xīngqīsān	Wednesday
14	学	xué	to learn
15	真的	zhēn de	really

课文翻译
TRANSLATION OF TEXTS

Unit 1

Lesson One

Liu Shaohua	I'm Liu Shaohua.
Zhao Yulan	I'm Zhao Yulan.
Mike	I'm Mike.
Zhang Fangfang	I'm Zhang Fangfang.
Zhang Yuanyuan	I'm Zhang Yuanyuan.
Kim Taesung	I'm Kim Taesung.
Yamaguchi Kazuko	I'm Yamaguchi Kazuko.
Wang Yang	I'm Wang Yang.
Mary	I'm Mary.
Faye	I'm Faye.
Li Dongsheng	I'm Li Dongsheng.
Chen Xiaohong	I'm Chen Xiaohong.

Lesson Two

At the registration office for international students.

Mike	Hello! I'm Mike.
Kim Taesung	Hello! I'm Kim Taesung.
Mary	Hello! I'm Mary.
Faye	Hello! I'm Faye.

In the classroom.

Li Dongsheng	Hello, everyone! I'm Li Dongsheng.

Lesson Three

In the classroom.

Mike	Hello! I'm Mike.
Mary	Hello! I'm Mary.

Faye comes into the classroom.

Mike	Who is she?
Mary	She is Faye.
Mike	Hello, Faye!
Faye	Hello!

Li Dongsheng comes into the classroom.

Li Dongsheng	Hello, everyone!
Mary	Who is he?
Faye	He is Teacher Li.
Mary	Hello, Teacher! I'm Mary.
Mike	Hello, Teacher! I'm Mike.
Li Dongsheng	Hello, Mike! Hello, Mary!

Unit 2

Lesson One

At the lobby of an apartment building. Kim Taesung comes in.

Kim Taesung	Hello!
Mike, Mary	Hello!
Mary	You are…?
Mike	He is Kim Taesung.
Kim Taesung	What's your name?
Mary	My name is Mary.

Lesson Two

At the entrance to the library, Kim Taesung bumped against Yamaguchi Kazuko accidentally and knocked the books out from her arms.

Kim Taesung	I'm sorry!
Yamaguchi Kazuko	Never mind! Hmm... are you a student?
Kim Taesung	Yes, I am.
Yamaguchi Kazuko	What's your surname?
Kim Taesung	My surname is Kim. My full name is Kim Taesung. May I ask what's your name?
Yamaguchi Kazuko	My name is Yamaguchi Kazuko.
Kim Taesung	It's nice to meet you.
Yamaguchi Kazuko	It's nice to meet you, too.

Lesson Three

At the cafeteria on campus. Mary and Kim Taesung are having their meal when Faye comes in.

Faye	Hello, Mary!
Mary	Hello!
Kim Taesung	What's her name?
Mary	Faye. Let me introduce. This is Faye. His surname is Kim. He is called Kim Taesung.
Faye	It's nice to meet you.
Kim Taesung	It's nice to meet you, too.

Unit 3

Lesson One

At the customs. Rawson is getting through the customs.

Customs officer	Hello, your name please?
Rawson	Pardon me. What's that?
Customs officer	What's your name?
Rawson	Rawson.
Customs officer	Nationality?
Rawson	I beg your pardon.
Customs officer	What's your nationality, please?
Rawson	French.
Customs officer	Oh, French. Your passport, please.
Rawson	Here you go.
Customs officer	Thanks!

Lesson Two

Yamaguchi Kazuko, Mary and Kim Taesung are chatting during the class break.

Yamguchi Kazuko	Hello, I'm Yamaguchi Kazuko.
Mary	Hello, I'm Mary.
Yamguchi Kazuko	Are you American?
Mary	No, I'm British. And you?
Yamguchi Kazuko	I'm Japanese.

Kim Taesung joins in.

Kim Taesung	Hello!
Mary	Hello, Kim Taesung. Are you also Japanese?
Kim Taesung	No, I'm not. I'm Korean.

Lesson Three

At a coffeehouse. Li Dongsheng and the students are chatting.

Faye	Teacher, where are you from?
Li Dongsheng	I'm from Beijing.
Yamaguchi Kazuko	Are your parents from Beijing, too?
Li Dongsheng	No. My father is from Shanghai. My mother is from Guangdong. Yamaguchi, which place in Japan are you from?
Yamaguchi Kazuko	I'm from Tokyo.
Li Dongsheng	Mary, where are you from?
Mary	I'm from London, UK. However my mother isn't from London. My mother's mother is Chinese.
Li Dongsheng	Oh?

Unit 4

Lesson One

In the gymnasium. Mike and the students are talking about their occupations.

Mike	Hi, everybody! I'm the coach. My name is Mike. I'm American.
Student 1	I'm Jane, Australian. I'm a nurse.
Student 2	My surname is Li. I'm a university student. I'm Chinese.
Student 3	Helllo, everyone! I'm German. I work for a company as a secretary.
	…
Mike	Ok, glad to meet you all. Music!

Music starts

Lesson Two

At the lobby of the library. Kim Taesung and Yamaguchi Kazuko are chatting.

Yamaguchi Kazuko	Kim Taesung, do you come to the library every day?
Kim Taesung	No. I work every aftertoon.
Yamaguchi Kazuko	Where do you work?
Kim Taesung	I work for a Korean company. I'm a department manager. Do you work, too?
Yamaguchi Kazuko	Yes. I work for a Japanese company.
Kim Taesung	What do you do?
Yamaguchi Kazuko	I'm a clerk.

Lesson Three

At the apartment's balcony. Mary and Faye are talking about occupations.

Mary	Faye, what kind of work do you do?
Faye	I'm a reporter.
Mary	Do you like your job?
Faye	I like it very much. Mary, do you work?
Mary	I don't work now.
Faye	What do you like to do?
Mary	I like to paint.
Faye	Ah, you are a painter!

Unit 5

Lesson One

Mary sees a little boy.

Mary	Hi, little friend! What's your name?
Little boy	My name is Li Ming.
Mary	How old are you?
Little boy	Can you guess?
Mary	5?
Little boy	Wrong.
Mary	7?
Little boy	Wrong. I'm 6. Aunty, how old are you?
Mary	This is a secret.

Lesson Two

At the gymnasium. Mike is coaching the students on how to do an aerobic exercise when Zhang Yuanyuan comes in to sign up for aerobics.

Mike	1, 2, 3, 4, 5, 6, 7, 8; 2, 2, 3, 4…
Zhang Yuanyuan	Hello, Coach!
Mike	Hello! What's up?
Zhang Yuanyuan	I'd like to join the gym.
Mike	What's your name? How old are you?
Zhang Yuanyuan	My name is Zhang Yuanyuan. I'm 21.
Mike	Zhang Yuanyuan, female, 21. OK, can you come over on

	Saturday morning?
Zhang Yuanyuan	OK!

Lesson Three
Mary is watching some seniors practising Peking opera outside a Siheyuan.

Mary	Aunt, is this Peking opera?
Elder 1	Yes, it is.
Mary	You have a beautiful voice! May I ask how old you are?
Elder 1	I'm 65. You are…?
Mary	I'm Mary from the UK. Do you know this person?
Elder 1	Who is she?
Mary	She is my mother's mother.
Elder 1	Oh, your maternal grandma. How old is she?
Mary	83 years old.
Elder 1	83… Come to have a look. Do you know this person?
Number of old	No, we don't. We don't.
Zhao Yulan	Let me have a look…

Unit 6

Lesson One
At the coffeehouse. Zhang Fangfang and Zhang Yuanyuan are talking about the coach in the gymnasium.

Zhang Fangfang	How's your coach?
Zhang Yuanyuan	Not bad. He is a foreigner. He's learning Chinese in a university.
Zhang Fangfang	A Foreigner? Man or woman?
Zhang Yuanyuan	A man, very tall.
Zhang Fangfang	How tall?
Zhang Yuanyuan	About 1.80 meters tall.
Zhang Fangfang	Is he handsome?
Zhang Yuanyuan	Very handsome.
Zhang Fangfang	Are you looking for a boyfriend like him?
Zhang Yuanyuan	What?

Lesson Two
Zhang Yuanyuan is doing exercises in the gymnasium when Mike comes over.

Mike	Miss Zhang. Are you tired?
Zhang Yuanyuan	No, I'm not.
Mike	Why don't you take a break tomorrow?
Zhang Yuanyuan	No. I want to come. I'm overweight.
Mike	You are NOT!
Zhang Yuanyuan	I weigh 54 kg.
Mike	That's OK. How tall are you?
Zhang Yuanyuan	1.65m.
Mike	1.65m, 54 kg. You are not overweight.

Lesson Three
At the apartment's balcony. Mary is showing Faye a picture and telling Faye about her grandmother.

Faye	Who is she?
Mary	My maternal grandma. She was 18 then.
Faye	She was so beautiful! Is she Chinese?
Mary	Yes. She is from Beijing.
Faye	And your maternal grandpa?
Mary	My maternal grandpa is British.
Faye	Ah.

Unit 7

Lesson One
In the gymnasium. Zhang Yuanyuan asks Mike to work as a callisthenics coach at her university.

Zhang Yuanyuan	Coach, there's an aerobics competition at my school.
Mike	Really? Will you join?
Zhang Yuanyuan	Yes, I will. Can you be our coach?
Mike	Good! I would also like to see your school.
Zhang Yuanyuan	Can you come tomorrow?
Mike	Yes, I'll go looking for you. Where do you live?
Zhang Yuanyuan	I live in Room 302, Student Residence Building 3. My telephone number is 82194675.
Mike	OK, see you tomorrow.

Lesson Two

Kim Taesung is talking to Wang Yang on the phone, inviting her to attend a banquet.

Kim Taesung	13682475099, hello, is this Wang Yang? I'm Kim Taesung. Where are you now?
Wang Yang	Hello, Manager Kim. I'm at home.
Kim Taesung	There's a banquet this evening. Why don't you join us?
Wang Yang	Where is it?
Kim Taesung	At Chang'an Hotel. I'm coming over to pick you up. Where do you live?
Wang Yang	I live in Yangguang Residential Neighborhood.
Kim Taesung	Which building?
Wang Yang	Room 1708, 17th Floor, Building 24.
Kim Taesung	Ok. I'll be waiting for you in front of Building 24. See you soon.

Lesson Three

At the intersection. Mary is asking a policeman about the location of a hospital.

Mary	Excuse me, where is No.2 Hospital?
Policeman	No.2 Hospital?
Mary	Yes.
Policeman	It's at No.15 Dongcheng Road.
Mary	Is it far from here?
Policeman	Not too far. Do you know Chang'an Hotel?
Mary	Yes, I do.
Policeman	No.2 Hospital is to the east of Chang'an Hotel.
Mary	Thank you.
Policeman	You are welcome.

Unit 8

Lesson One

At the lobby of an apartment building. Mary is looking at her grandmother's picture.

Faye	Missing your maternal grandma?
Mary	Yes. My mother said my maternal grandma is in Beijing.
Faye	How many people are there in your family?
Mary	Four. My father, my mother, my younger sister and me.
Faye	Oh, you have a younger sister! How old is she?
Mary	She's 18, and she's a university student.
Faye	What does your father do?
Mary	He's a lawyer. He's very busy. He's not at home often.
Faye	Does your mother work, too?
Mary	Yes, she works, too. She's a teacher.

Lesson Two

At the coffeehouse. Zhang Yuanyuan and Mike are chatting.

Zhang Yuanyuan	Mike, did you work in America?
Mike	No, I didn't. My father hoped that I could work in a bank, but I didn't like that.
Zhang Yuanyuan	What does your father do?
Mike	He's a doctor.
Zhang Yuanyuan	Do you have any brothers or sisters?
Mike	I'm the only child in my family. What about you?
Zhang Yuanyuan	I have an elder sister.
Mike	How old is she?
Zhang Yuanyuan	She's 21, too. We're twins.
Mike	She's also beautiful, isn't she?

Lesson Three

After the banquet. Kim Taesung drives Wang Yang back to Yangguang Residential Neighborhood.

Wang Yang	The Yangguang Residential Neighborhood is just ahead of us. Thank you for escorting me.
Kim Taesung	This residential community is really beautiful. Do you live alone?
Wang Yang	No. I live with my parents. And you?
Kim Taesung	I live alone now. My family are all still in Republic of Korea.
Wang Yang	What people are there in your family?
Kim Taesung	My grandpa, grandma, father, mother and my elder brother, his wife, and their kids, altogether 10 people.
Wang Yang	That's really a big family. Do you all live together?
Kim Taesung	Yes, we all live together.

Unit 9

Lesson One

Mary is drawing a picture in a park when some tourists come over and ask her about the time.

Tourist 1	Excuse me, may I ask what time is it now?
Mary	It's 10:20.
Tourist 2	Excuse me, what time is it?
Mary	It's 10:30.
Tourist 3	Excuse me, what time is it?
Mary	It's already 10:50.
Tourist 4	Excuse me, what time is it?
Mary	It's 11:05.

Mary puts up a piece of paper: I don't know what time it is!

45 minutes later.

Tourist 5	Young lady, it's ten to twelve now.
Mary	...

Lesson Two

At the drill ground of the university. Mike and Zhang Yuanyuan are discussing the time for their training.

Zhang Yuanyuan	So what do you think?
Mike	Not bad. I'm willing to be your coach.
Zhang Yuanyuan	Can you come over tomorrow?
Mike	What time?
Zhang Yuanyuan	How about 3 p.m.?
Mike	I start to work at 3 p.m. and finish at 5:30. How about 6?
Zhang Yuanyuan	6 isn't OK. We have dinner from 5:30 to 6:30.
Mike	Then I'll come over at 7. We

Zhang Yuanyuan	can start training at 7:30. That's wonderful. Thank you!

Lesson Three

At the cafeteria on campus. Yamaguchi Kazuko and Kim Taesung are talking about their daily routines.

Yamaguchi Kazuko	Mr Kim, you must be very busy recently?
Kim Taesung	Yes, I am. I get up at 6 a.m. every day, and go to bed after 12 midnight.
Yamaguchi Kazuko	So busy?
Kim Taesung	I study Chinese in the morning, amd work for the company in the afternoon. And recently I have to work overtime in the evening.
Yamaguchi Kazuko	Work overtime?
Kim Taesung	Yes. The head office has assigned me a very important task.
Yamaguchi Kazuko	What time do you usually get off work every day?
Kim Taesung	There is no set time. Sometimes at 8 p.m., and sometimes at 10 p.m..
Yamaguchi Kazuko	I'd like to have dinner with you. Do you have time this Friday night?
Kim Taesung	Let's see.

Unit 10

Lesson One

At the coffeehouse. Zhang Yuanyuan is introducing Mike to Zhang Fangfang.

Zhang Yuanyuan	Fangfang, let me do the introductions. This is Mike, my coach in the gymnasium. Mike, this is my elder sister, Zhang Fangfang.
Mike	Hello, Fangfang. Glad to meet you.
Zhang Fangfang	Hi, Mike. (turning to Yuanyuan and speaking in soft voice) He's really handsome!
Mike	What did you say?
Zhang Yuanyuan	Nothing, nothing. Fangfang also wants to join the gym.
Mike	Most welcome. You may go to the gym together.
Zhang Fangfang	When are you going to the gym next time?
Zhang Yuanyuan	3:30 p.m. Wednesday.
Zhang Fangfang	OK. We'll go together.

Lesson Two

At the campus gate. Faye comes across Li Dongsheng and Chen Xiaohong.

Faye	Hello, Teacher Li!
Li Dongsheng	Hello! Let me do the introductions. This is Faye, my student. This is Chen Xiaohong, Teacher Chen.
Faye	Hello, Teacher Chen!
Chen Xiaohong	Hello, Faye! What's your nationality?
Faye	I'm Indonesian.
Chen Xiaohong	Do you live on campus?
Faye	Yes, I live at Room 433, Building 6. Teacher Chen, do you also teach Chinese?
Chen Xiaohong	No. I teach French.
Faye	Are you friends?
Li Dongsheng	Yes. She's my teacher's daughter.
Faye	Oh.

Lesson Three

At the drama rehearsal room. The artist Zhao Yulan and Mary are chatting.

Mary	Teacher Zhao, how old are you?
Zhao Yulan	I'm 48. And you?
Mary	22. I want to learn Peking opera. Can you teach me?
Zhao Yulan	OK!
Mary	When are you free?
Zhao Yulan	I'm free every afternoon.
Mary	I have no classes in the afternoon. I'll give you a call.
Zhao Yulan	Sure. My phone number is 61794277.
Mary	67194727.
Zhao Yulan	It's 61794277.

词语表
VOCABULARY LIST

A

阿姨	āyí	aunty	Unit 5
啊	à	aha (used to express sudden realization)	Unit 4
啊	a	ah (modal particle)	Unit 6
澳大利亚	Àodàlìyà	Australia	Unit 4

B

爸爸	bàba	dad, father	Unit 3
吧	ba	a particle (used at the end of a question)	Unit 3
半	bàn	half	Unit 9
北京	Běijīng	Beijing	Unit 3
比赛	bǐsài	competition	Unit 7
遍	biàn	(measure word, mainly used for the times of actions)	Unit 3
别	bié	don't	Unit 7
别客气	bié kèqi	you are welcome	Unit 7
不	bù	no, not	Unit 3
不错	búcuò	not bad	Unit 6
不一定	bùyídìng	not sure	Unit 9
部门	bùmén	department	Unit 4
部门经理	bùmén jīnglǐ	department manager	Unit 4

C

猜	cāi	to guess	Unit 5
参加	cānjiā	to participate in	Unit 7
层	céng	floor of a building	Unit 7
差	chà	to be less than, to be short of	Unit 9
长安饭店	Cháng'ān Fàndiàn	Chang'an Hotel	Unit 7
常常	chángcháng	often	Unit 8
陈晓红	Chén Xiǎohóng	Chen Xiaohong	Unit 1
吃	chī	to eat	Unit 9
次	cì	time (measure word)	Unit 10
从	cóng	from	Unit 3

D

打	dǎ	to make (a phone call)	Unit 10
大	dà	old; big	Unit 5
大家	dàjiā	everybody	Unit 4
大妈	dàmā	aunt	Unit 5
大学	dàxué	university	Unit 6
大学生	dàxuéshēng	college student	Unit 4
但	dàn	but	Unit 3
当	dāng	to act as, to serve as	Unit 7
到	dào	to arrive, to reach	Unit 9
德国	Déguó	Germany	Unit 4

——*The colored words are proper nouns.——

Vocabulary List

的	de	(used with an adjective or attribute phrase; indicating a possessive relationship)	Unit 3
等	děng	to wait, to expect	Unit 7
地方	dìfang	place	Unit 3
第	dì	(used before numerals to form ordinal numbers)	Unit 7
第二	dì-èr	the second	Unit 7
第二医院	Dì-èr Yīyuàn	No. 2 Hospital	Unit 7
点	diǎn	o'clock, hour (measure word)	Unit 9
电话	diànhuà	telephone	Unit 7
东边	dōngbian	the east	Unit 7
东城路	Dōngchéng Lù	Dongcheng Road	Unit 7
东京	Dōngjīng	Tokyo	Unit 3
都	dōu	all	Unit 8
对	duì	correct, right	Unit 5
对不起	duìbuqǐ	I'm sorry	Unit 2
多	duō	how	Unit 5
多大	duō dà	how old	Unit 5

E

| 二 | èr | two | Unit 7 |

F

法国	Fǎguó	France	Unit 3
饭店	fàndiàn	hotel, restaurant	Unit 7
房间	fángjiān	room	Unit 7
非常	fēicháng	very, extremely	Unit 8
菲雅	Fēiyǎ	Faye	Unit 1
分	fēn	minute (measure word)	Unit 9
父母	fùmǔ	parents	Unit 8

G

高	gāo	tall	Unit 6
高兴	gāoxìng	happy	Unit 2
哥哥	gēge	elder brother	Unit 8
个	gè	(measure word)	Unit 4
个子	gèzi	stature, height	Unit 6
给	gěi	to give	Unit 3
给	gěi	to, for	Unit 10
工作	gōngzuò	to work	Unit 4
公斤	gōngjīn	kilogram (measure word)	Unit 6
公司	gōngsī	firm, company	Unit 4
姑娘	gūniang	young lady	Unit 9
广东	Guǎngdōng	Guangdong	Unit 3
贵姓	guìxìng	(your) surname (honorific)	Unit 2
国	guó	country, state	Unit 3
国籍	guójí	nationality	Unit 3

H

还	hái	yet, still	Unit 6
还是	háishi	or	Unit 6
孩子	háizi	child	Unit 8
韩国	Hánguó	Republic of Korea	Unit 3
汉语	Hànyǔ	Chinese language	Unit 6
好	hǎo	well, good	Unit 1
好	hǎo	(used to express approval, conclusion, discontent, etc)	Unit 4
好的	hǎo de	OK	Unit 10
好听	hǎotīng	pleasant to hear, sound nice	Unit 5
号	hào	number, order	Unit 7
和	hé	and	Unit 8

www.greatwallchinese.com 133

Great Wall Chinese

很	hěn	very, quite	Unit 2
护士	hùshi	nurse	Unit 4
护照	hùzhào	passport	Unit 3
画	huà	to paint, to draw; painting, drawing	Unit 4
画家	huàjiā	painter, artist	Unit 4
欢迎	huānyíng	to welcome	Unit 10

J

几	jǐ	how many; several	Unit 5
记者	jìzhě	reporter	Unit 4
加班	jiābān	to work overtime	Unit 9
家	jiā	(measure word)	Unit 4
家	jiā	home, family	Unit 7
家庭	jiātíng	family	Unit 8
见	jiàn	to meet, to see	Unit 7
健美操	jiànměicāo	callisthenics	Unit 7
健身	jiànshēn	to keep fit	Unit 5
教	jiāo	to teach	Unit 10
教练	jiàoliàn	coach	Unit 4
叫	jiào	to be called as	Unit 2
接	jiē	to pick up	Unit 7
姐姐	jiějie	elder sister	Unit 8
姐妹	jiěmèi	sisters	Unit 8
介绍	jièshào	to introduce	Unit 2
今年	jīnnián	this year	Unit 5
今天	jīntiān	today	Unit 7
金太成	Jīn Tàichéng	Kim Taesung	Unit 1
京剧	jīngjù	Peking opera	Unit 5
经理	jīnglǐ	manager	Unit 4
就	jiù	just	Unit 8

K

开始	kāishǐ	to start	Unit 9
看	kàn	to take a look	Unit 5
可是	kěshì	but	Unit 8
可以	kěyǐ	can, may	Unit 5
可以	kěyǐ	passable, not bad	Unit 6
客气	kèqi	to be polite	Unit 7
课	kè	lesson, class	Unit 10
口	kǒu	(measure word, used for family members)	Unit 8

L

来	lái	(used before a verb or a verbal expression, indicating an intended action)	Unit 2
来	lái	to come	Unit 3
劳驾	láojià	excuse me	Unit 9
老师	lǎoshī	teacher	Unit 1
累	lèi	tired, fatigued	Unit 6
离	lí	to be away from	Unit 7
李冬生	Lǐ Dōngshēng	Li Dongsheng	Unit 1
李明	Lǐ Míng	Li Ming	Unit 5
里	li	in (used after nouns and some monosyllabic adjectives to indicate place, time, limit, direction, etc)	Unit 7
刘少华	Liú Shàohuá	Liu Shaohua	Unit 1
楼	lóu	building	Unit 7
路	lù	road	Unit 7
律师	lùshī	lawyer	Unit 8
伦敦	Lúndūn	London	Unit 3
罗森	Luósēn	Rawson	Unit 3

M

妈妈	māma	mom, mother	Unit 3
玛丽	Mǎlì	Mary	Unit 1
吗	ma	(a particle used at	Unit 2

Vocabulary List

		the end of a question)	
麦克	Màikè	Mike	Unit 1
忙	máng	busy	Unit 8
没关系	méi guānxi	it doesn't matter	Unit 2
没什么	méi shénme	nothing	Unit 10
没有	méiyǒu	not to have, to be without	Unit 10
每	měi	every, each	Unit 4
每天	měi tiān	every day	Unit 4
美国	Měiguó	United States of America (USA)	Unit 3
妹妹	mèimei	younger sister	Unit 8
米	mǐ	meter (measure word)	Unit 6
秘密	mìmì	secret	Unit 5
秘书	mìshū	secretary	Unit 4
名	míng	(measure word)	Unit 4
名字	míngzi	name	Unit 2
明天	míngtiān	tomorrow	Unit 6

N

哪	nǎ	which; where	Unit 3
哪儿	nǎr	where	Unit 4
那时	nàshí	then, at that time	Unit 6
奶奶	nǎinai	grandma	Unit 8
男	nán	male	Unit 6
男朋友	nán péngyou	boyfriend	Unit 6
呢	ne	(auxiliary word)	Unit 8
能	néng	to be able to	Unit 9
嗯	ńg	eh (expressing question)	Unit 2
你	nǐ	you	Unit 1
你们	nǐmen	you (plural form)	Unit 1
年纪	niánjì	age	Unit 5
您	nín	you (polite form)	Unit 1
女	nǚ	female	Unit 5
女儿	nǚ'ér	daughter	Unit 10

O

哦	ó	oh (expressing doubt)	Unit 3
哦	ò	oh (expressing realization and understanding)	Unit 3

P

胖	pàng	overweight	Unit 6
朋友	péngyou	friend	Unit 10
漂亮	piàoliang	pretty	Unit 6

Q

起床	qǐchuáng	to get up	Unit 9
前边	qiánbian	front	Unit 7
前面	qiánmiàn	front	Unit 8
请	qǐng	please	Unit 2
请问	qǐngwèn	may I ask…	Unit 2
去	qù	to go to	Unit 7

R

人	rén	people, person	Unit 3
认识	rènshi	to know	Unit 2
日本	Rìběn	Japan	Unit 3

S

嫂子	sǎozi	sister-in-law (wife of your elder brother)	Unit 8
山口和子	Shānkǒu Hézǐ	Yamaguchi Kazuko	Unit 1
上班	shàngbān	to go to work	Unit 9
上海	Shànghǎi	Shanghai	Unit 3
上午	shàngwǔ	morning, am	Unit 5
什么	shénme	what	Unit 2

声音	shēngyīn	voice	Unit 5
时候	shíhou	time, moment	Unit 9
时间	shíjiān	time	Unit 10
是	shì	to be	Unit 1
事	shì	business, matter	Unit 5
帅	shuài	handsome	Unit 6
双胞胎	shuāngbāotāi	twins	Unit 8
谁	shéi	who	Unit 1
睡觉	shuìjiào	to sleep	Unit 9
说	shuō	to say, to speak	Unit 3
四	sì	four	Unit 8
送	sòng	to escort	Unit 8
宿舍	sùshè	dormitory	Unit 7
岁	suì	(measure word, used for age)	Unit 5

T

他	tā	he, him	Unit 1
他们	tāmen	they	Unit 8
她	tā	she, her	Unit 1
太	tài	too	Unit 6
体重	tǐzhòng	weight	Unit 6
天	tiān	day	Unit 4
图书馆	túshūguǎn	library	Unit 4

W

外公	wàigōng	grandfather	Unit 6
外国	wàiguó	foreign country	Unit 6
外国人	wàiguó rén	foreigner	Unit 6
外婆	wàipó	grandmother	Unit 5
晚饭	wǎnfàn	supper	Unit 9
晚上	wǎnshang	evening	Unit 7
王杨	Wáng Yáng	Wang Yang	Unit 1
喂	wèi	hello	Unit 7
问	wèn	to ask	Unit 2

我	wǒ	I, me	Unit 1
我们	wǒmen	we, us	Unit 7

X

希望	xīwàng	to hope, to wish	Unit 8
喜欢	xǐhuan	to like	Unit 4
下	xià	next	Unit 10
下班	xiàbān	to be off duty, to get off work	Unit 9
下次	xià cì	next time	Unit 10
下午	xiàwǔ	afternoon	Unit 4
先生	xiānsheng	Mr	Unit 9
现在	xiànzài	now	Unit 4
想	xiǎng	to want	Unit 5
项	xiàng	(measure word)	Unit 9
小姐	xiǎojiě	miss	Unit 6
小朋友	xiǎopéngyǒu	little friend	Unit 5
小区	xiǎoqū	residential neighborhood	Unit 7
谢谢	xièxie	to thank	Unit 3
星期六	Xīngqīliù	Saturday	Unit 5
星期三	Xīngqīsān	Wednesday	Unit 10
星期五	Xīngqīwǔ	Friday	Unit 9
行	xíng	will do	Unit 9
姓	xìng	to be surnamed	Unit 2
姓名	xìngmíng	name	Unit 3
兄弟	xiōngdì	brothers	Unit 8
兄弟姐妹	xiōngdì jiěmèi	brothers and sisters	Unit 8
休息	xiūxi	to have a rest	Unit 6
学	xué	to learn	Unit 10
学生	xuéshēng	student	Unit 2
学习	xuéxí	to learn	Unit 6
学校	xuéxiào	school; university	Unit 7
训练	xùnliàn	to train	Unit 9

Y

宴会	yànhuì	banquet	Unit 7
阳光	Yángguāng	Yangguang	Unit 7
小区	Xiǎoqū	Residential Neighborhood	
爷爷	yéye	grandpa	Unit 8
要	yào	to want (to do)	Unit 6
也	yě	too, also, as well	Unit 2
一	yī	one	Unit 3
一共	yígòng	altogether	Unit 8
一会儿	yíhuìr	a little while	Unit 7
一下	yíxià	one time, once (used after a verb as its complement, indicating an act or an attempt)	Unit 2
一起	yìqǐ	together	Unit 8
医生	yīshēng	doctor	Unit 8
医院	yīyuàn	hospital	Unit 7
以后	yǐhòu	later, after	Unit 9
银行	yínháng	bank	Unit 8
英国	Yīngguó	United Kingdom (UK)	Unit 3
有	yǒu	there be; to have	Unit 7
有空儿	yǒu kòngr	to be free	Unit 9
有时候	yǒushíhou	sometimes, occasionally	Unit 9
远	yuǎn	far	Unit 7
愿意	yuànyì	to be willing to	Unit 9

Z

再	zài	again, once more	Unit 3
再说	zàishuō	to put off until some time later	Unit 9
在	zài	at, in, on	Unit 4
怎么样	zěnmeyàng	how	Unit 6
张芳芳	Zhāng Fāngfāng	Zhang Fangfang	Unit 1
张圆圆	Zhāng Yuányuan	Zhang Yuanyuan	Unit 1
找	zhǎo	to look for	Unit 6
赵玉兰	Zhào Yùlán	Zhao Yulan	Unit 1
这	zhè	this	Unit 5
这儿	zhèr	here	Unit 7
这个	zhège	this one	Unit 4
这么	zhème	such, so	Unit 9
这样	zhèyàng	such, like this	Unit 6
珍妮	Zhēnní	Jane	Unit 4
真	zhēn	really	Unit 5
真的	zhēn de	really	Unit 10
知道	zhīdào	to know	Unit 7
职员	zhíyuán	clerk	Unit 4
只	zhǐ	only	Unit 8
中国	Zhōngguó	China	Unit 3
重要	zhòngyào	important	Unit 9
住	zhù	to live	Unit 7
总公司	zǒnggōngsī	head office	Unit 9
最近	zuìjìn	lately, recently	Unit 9
左右	zuǒyòu	about, or so (used after a number)	Unit 6
做	zuò	to do, to make	Unit 4